D1104064

Looking at
CHINESE PAINTING

Text by **Wang Yao-t'ing**

Translated by The Stone Studio

Looking at CHINESE PAINTING
text by Wang Yao-t'ing
translated by The Stone Studio

English edition: February 1996
Published by Nigensha Publishing Co Ltd.
2-2, Kanda Jimbocho, Chiyoda-ku, Tokyo, 101 JAPAN

Printed and bound in Hong Kong

ISBN4-544-02066-2

Japanese first edition:
©Nigensha Publishing Co Ltd, 1995

All rights reserved
No part of this publication may be reproduced or transmitted,
in any form or by any means, without permission.

A NOTE ON THE DECORATIONS. The back of the jacket and the inside cover
show details from the following work reproduced with negative contrast effect.
Li Sung, Sung dynasty: Basket of Flowers.
The National Palace Musuem, Taipei

Looking at
CHINESE PAINTING

Table of Contents

Part One
A View to Chinese Painting

Part Two
An Introduction to the History of Chinese Painting

Anonymous, Sung dynasty: Cat under the peonies.

Preface

Whether it is a beautiful painting one faces in a museum or gallery, or a fine reproduction that one finds leafing through a book in the comfort of one's own living room, should a certain interest be sensed, a certain measure of contentment in looking, then one is already experiencing the pleasure of appreciation.

Since ancient times in China, one phrase in particular has been used to describe the painter's creativity: "Outwardly one learns from the Creator; inwardly one plumbs the source of one's heart." This can be explained as meaning the painter gains insight and inspiration from what is seen and heard and relies upon superior faculties to produce an excellent work of art. We also often say that an exceptional painting is full of life and that it is capable of expressing to the viewer the painter's feelings and thoughts. Conversely, the subtleties of a work of art must be discerned by the viewer if all of the beauty the artist invests in it is to be conveyed. It matters little if the beauty of a painting is born from the personal vision of an artist or from a more objective, universal standard. How exactly a painting is to be interpreted may be a matter of debate, but the very fact that it can elicit the praise of many is proof that in terms of aesthetic appreciation, there exists a sphere of collective agreement.

There is no avoiding the fact that when looking at a given work of art, various kinds of interpretation are possible. These include scientific analysis based on careful observation of fact, criticism arising from superlative reasoning, judgments of quality born from nothing more than one's personal feelings, or perhaps a combination of these three approaches. Yet, there are even more people who would frankly admit their inability to understand what it is that a painting expresses. Painting is a visual art. Be it traditional Chinese style painting or Western painting, form and color are the means of expression. Form and color are not like the language of words, which is studied by all, recognized by all, and whose meaning in a given context allows little divergence of interpretation. From the time we are children, we all learn how to use verbal language to communicate our thoughts and feelings, but when it comes to the understanding of form and color, few ever make much effort, outside of the specialist and occasional enthusiast. Confucius once said that one can look without seeing. How is it that looking is not the same as seeing? When viewing a painting, we look at its various forms and colors and we wish to understand what these things tell us. It is at this moment that we must ask what is the proper way of looking.

What can be done to increase one's ability to appreciate Chinese painting? An anecdote recorded in *Meng-ch'i pi-t'an* by the eleventh century scholar Shen Kua reflects upon this question. In the collection of Ou-yang Hsiu was an old painting of a bush of flowering peonies with a cat underneath. No one in the Ou-yang family was able to judge the painting's quality, but a relative by marriage surnamed Wu formed an opinion immediately after seeing it. "This painting depicts that moment at high noon," he said. "One knows this from the fact that the petals are fully open, their color ripe but with a hint of dryness. Moreover, the cat's pupils are reduced to slivers, precisely as one sees at this time of the day." This was a viewer who had the insight to intuit the artist's ability to capture the characteristics of a moment in time. The point of the story is that both painter and viewer can possess remarkable powers of observation.

The tasks of the painter and viewer are essentially the same: to examine with diligence the expressive capabilities of a subject. While Chinese landscape painters rarely paint *en plein air*, it is only after many years spent experiencing first-hand the wonders of nature that a deep intuitive understanding develops and the ability to express it through art. At the turn of the eleventh century, the great landscape painter Fan K'uan lived deep in the mountains and studied his surroundings ceaselessly, seeking the characteristics of mountains and rivers in their seasonal transformations. Even in the frozen grip of winter, he would wander about observing, seeking inspiration for his painting. A century later, the Sung dynasty emperor Hui-tsung ordered his court academy painters to note carefully how the peacock, when surmounting the terrace, always steps first with its left foot. It is only after such moments of penetrating observation that the excellent artist can convey his subject's forms and colors.

If the viewer can learn some of the characteristics of the historical development of Chinese painting, and for that matter, some of the fundamental principles of painting in general, he or she will make great progress in understanding the subtleties of this wonderful art. It is the goal of this book to aid the viewer in setting out on this path to understanding Chinese painting.

The book is divided into two parts, with part one addressing the important issue of appreciation. Through the long history of China, a considerable amount of experience was gained through the critical evaluation of Chinese painting—what can be considered the crystallization of a culture's knowledge. In the sixth century, for example, Hsieh Ho of the Ch'i dynasty arranged and ordered the viewpoints of earlier writers and formulated his Six Laws of Painting, which have been quoted frequently to the present day. Each period of Chinese history since has provided a rich sampling of writings on painting—bits and pieces of wisdom from the luminaries of yesteryear. In our discussion of the appreciation of Chinese painting, naturally we base ourselves first in tradition. At the same time, however, we should recognize the benefits of our own century. Modern printing, for example, allows us to circumvent the most daunting of obstacles of the past, which was the opportunity to view a painting directly. A painting is something to be seen, not heard about, and if we cannot approach it, there is no way we can touch upon its essential character. Our eyes must provide the standard; relying on the words of others will not do. In this book, plates and figures accompany all discussion so that the reader will be able to see the points being made. Modern printing techniques may not be able to match the experience of viewing a painting firsthand, but they provide us with an excellent substitute—one step shy of having the real item before our eyes. In this regard, our opportunities for understanding traditional painting are much better than those of our ancestors.

Su Shih described Mount Lu with the following words: "Abreast it forms a mountain range, from the side it becomes a peak." It is no different when it comes to looking at a painting—different viewpoints result in different impressions. In this book's step-by-step analysis of traditional Chinese painting, we begin with the concept of "viewing" itself. We wish to know how the painter viewed nature and how he adopted the elements of nature to create a landscape. When the process by which a painting is made is understood, it becomes easier to understand the artist's intentions. Next we look at the painting as an overall unit: its composition and use of solids and voids. Painting is, at root, forms and colors. We thus follow with a discussion of brush techniques and color. Monochrome ink painting is a special feature of Chinese painting; so special that discussion is often reduced to the two elements of brush and ink. The traditional writing brush is the primary tool of Chinese art. As calligraphy and painting share numerous points in common, both in terms of technique and aesthetics, this will certainly be worthy of discussion. Moreover, poetry is often combined with these two to form a single integrated unit. Like calligraphy, poetry has long been considered to be a sister art of painting. Two chapters will discuss these relationships. Inscriptions, seals and formats of mounting, all important elements of Chinese painting, will also be introduced. Two more characteristics of Chinese painting will be addressed. The first is the idea of painting as play, which pertains to a category of traditional painting that is quite distinct from the more orthodox forms guided by well-established rules. This chapter is intended to broaden the viewer's outlook; quality in painting is what is important, not its manner of expression. Authenticity is another interesting question, one that follows naturally after appreciation. One chapter will introduce to the reader this issue as it pertains to Chinese painting. The second half of the book provides a brief history of Chinese painting. From early antiquity to the late Ch'ing dynasty, there is a continuous, related development. I hope that beyond appreciation, the reader will also come to understand the mutual relationships between painters that form the fabric of Chinese painting history.

For many years I have been engaged in work related to teaching about Chinese painting. I hope that this book will help guide the reader into this vast and fertile world.

Wang Yao-t'ing

Part One

A View to Chinese Painting

1 Ch'iu Ying, Ming dynasty:
Pavilions in the Deep Mountains.

(detail *left*)

Chapter One
Where Do We Search for the Pavilions of Immortal Mountains?
The Viewpoint in Traditional Chinese Painting

Figure 1 illustrates "Pavilions in the Deep Mountains," painted by the Ming dynasty artist Ch'iu Ying. Distant mountains sharply rise like bamboo shoots of stone, their waists enwrapped by languid, curling clouds. At the lower left of the painting is a small flat slope with thin, graceful pine trees. Across in the distance is a spacious pavilion. Along the right border of the painting, hugging the base of the mountains above the water, is a covered causeway that leads to a gem-like building complex. It is a lovely scene well-described by the painting's title and we are compelled to ask, where does one begin to search for a realm such as this? If possible, one would turn back the clock four hundred years and ask Ch'iu Ying directly, but that is beyond our means.

Perhaps you may be startled by the spectacular scenery presented in Chinese landscape paintings and wonder if such places truly exist. The fact of the matter is Chinese paintings are not unlike the plots of novels, constructed of ideas, characters and situations that range from the totally fictitious to the partially or entirely true. In most cases, the borderline between fact and fiction is unclear.

1. Scenery and Idea-realms

Human affairs come and go while rivers and mountains are essentially changeless. The landscapes that inspired the painters of centuries ago are still visible today. Here are a few examples that will serve as a basis of comparison with painting. Located between Ho-hsien and T'ai-p'ing Prefectures in Anhui Province is Huang-shan (Yellow Mountain), renowned for its strange, twisted pines, bizarre rock formations, "sea of clouds" and hot springs. In the seventeenth century, during the late Ming and early Ch'ing dynasties, a number of Ming loyalist painters chose to live or travel in this area and adopted Huang-shan's unusual scenery as the raw material for their paintings. Among them are Shih-t'ao (1642-1707?), Mei Ch'ing (1623-97) and Chien-chiang (also known as Hung-jen, 1610-64). Let us first compare the monk Chien-chiang's painting "Pines and Rocks of the Yellow Sea," dated 1660, with a recent photograph of Huang-shan's famous "sleeping dragon" pine (figs. 2, 3). Passing birds drop seeds into the cracks and crevices of Huang-shan's bald rock faces and pine trees emerge. Their twisted roots grasp the sheer surfaces, and their forms, chiseled by centuries of wind and frost, become the very image of ancient strength. The scenery may not correspond exactly with what is seen in the photograph, but there is no question that Chien-chiang's painting was inspired by Huang-shan.

In the second example, we compare Mei Ch'ing's "Refining-

3 "Sleeping dragon" pine on Huangshan.

黄海松石

爲

文翁先生寫

2 Hung-jen, Ch'ing dynasty:
Pines and Rocks of the Yellow Sea.

Cinnabar Terrace of Huang-shan" with a photograph of the Manjusri Monastery (figs. 4, 5). In both painting and photograph, we note buildings atop seemingly unscalable precipices bathed in clouds and mist. The shapes of the mountain peaks differ—Mei Ch'ing's square and that which supports the Manjusri Monastery tapering—but the rich misty atmosphere is quite similar. No wonder people say that Chien-chiang paints a rock and a pine of Huang-shan while Mei Ch'ing captures the myriad transformations of its enchanting clouds.

5 Huangshan and Manjusri Monastery.

Of course, a painting is not the same as a photograph. In Chien-chiang's case, the artist chooses to reveal a world that is bright and unsoiled, crisp and bracing—characteristics that do not appear in the photograph. In opposite fashion, Mei Ch'ing's work is filled with a thick, palpable atmosphere. These two artists' manners could hardly be more different.

4 Mei-ch'ing, Ch'ing dynasty:
Refining-Cinnabar Terrace of Huangshan.

7 Top of Huashan.

It is, of course, entirely natural for a painter to adopt elements of landscape experienced firsthand and use these in one's painting. This was particularly so during the early period of landscape painting's development, when painters took verisimilitude as one of their goals and approached the landscape's scenery with an attitude of utmost respect. Let us see how Fan K'uan's "Travelers among Mountains and Streams" (fig. 6) fares in comparison to real landscape. Historical sources inform us that Fan K'uan resided in the region of Chung-nan and T'ai-hua, which is located in Shensi Province. There is little doubt that this famous work by Fan K'uan was inspired by Hua-shan, one of the five sacred peaks of China, located in Shensi. Comparing it with a photograph of Hua-shan (fig. 7), we see how the main peak of Fan K'uan's painting derived its awesome, impenetrable air from the sheer rock face of Hua-shan's massive range. Yet, taking this analysis a step further, we also come to recognize that Fan K'uan's painting consists of its own separate world, complete and personal. The view provided in the photograph, wide as it is and compellingly beautiful, can never provide the sense of completeness and unity that we sense in Fan K'uan's landscape. This is what has been called "the lofty and marvelous aspect of landscape" that exists in the painter's breast and is not something easily attained.

In traditional China, one often discussed painting in terms of the ancient, if amorphous, principle *ch'i-yun sheng-tung*, "breath-resonance generated by movement." Today it is more common to critique a painting's *i-ching*, or "idea-realm." *I-ching* is also a difficult term to understand, but it is somewhat less abstract than "breath-resonance." Facing a painting, the viewer will contemplate what it is the painter wishes to express. Chinese painters themselves commonly speak of "the idea being present before the brush descends." A painting is not a reproduction of nature's scenery and what differentiates it is precisely this—the painting's "idea." The painter's task is not simply to capture the outer form of his subject. It is even more important to grasp its spirit or essence and to make this visible to the viewer. When the painter contemplates a particular scene, feelings are born. Thoughts that are difficult to express through words arise and images are used instead. This merging of "scene" and "emotion" is precisely what is referred to by idea-realm. We can judge a painting's quality by whether or not ideas are present and their particular character if they are. Looking at the grand spectacle of Fan K'uan's work, the beguiling quality of Mei Ch'ing's clouds and the strange allure emanating from Chien-chiang's painting, the viewer intuits the painter's ideas and is filled with his or her own feelings.

Left
6 Fan K'uan, Sung dynasty:
Travelers among Mountains and Streams.

2. Composition and Viewpoint

Returning to the issue of what it is that differentiates Fan K'uan's "Travelers among Mountains and Streams" from the photograph of Hua-shan, we note the special character of the Chinese painter's approach to composition. The painter is able to transcend the limits of what the eye perceives, penetrate the subtleties of the subject and fashion a new world. The principle involved is one of selection and suggestion. While trees have four sides, only one angle needs to be shown. A painting can capture the ever-changing appearance of mountains as one travels through them, the depths of its canyons, but does not try to present all of the elements of an actual scene. The painter draws from his experiences with the famous mountains of China, their distant aspects, their interior subtleties, their climatic changes. He synthesizes and selects, all before the painting is begun.

Fan K'uan's painting again provides an example. The painting can be divided into three scenes: near, middle and distant. The near scene is comprised of the large boulders at the bottom of the composition and extends to the road traversed by the pack animals. The middle ground consists of the two rising slopes bisected by a forward-moving stream. The distant scene is the massif that rises abruptly from the mist. For the foreground scene, the painter adopted a slightly higher perspective than the boulders below so that their tops can be seen. Had he adopted the same prospect for the middle scene, however, we would only be able to see the tops of the rising slopes and not the slopes in their entirety. Moreover, we would be looking up at the eaves of the temple complex to the right and not be able to see the tilework on the roofs. Our elevation, in other words, has risen to a position higher than the temple. The scrubby trees atop the massif in the distance are also seen from above, so now our prospect is above the mountain peak. We conclude that Fan K'uan adopted three different perspectives in painting "Travelers among Mountains and Streams." No camera can perform the same trick.

In general, Chinese painting adopts a moving perspective. This is well illustrated by Fan K'uan's landscape. In constructing his scene, he utilized the mist formed by the cascade and water below to set the images off and add an element of spatial depth. The spatial limits of the painting are broken, the landscape is infused with atmosphere and the various scenes become harmoniously integrated. In this manner, the painter adopts different measures of composition and technique to convey his ideas.

When the differences between Chinese and Western painting are explored, it is often perspective that draws the most attention. This is an issue worth commenting upon. Earlier in this century, an element of self-criticism attended the influence of Western culture. Many considered traditional Chinese painting to be "unscientific," exemplified by what was considered to be the absence of perspective. In one well-known example, the painter Hsü Pei-hung (1895-1953) criticized a scene of "Admonitions of the Court Instructress" by the Tsin dynasty artist Ku K'ai-chih, in which a traditional Chinese bed is shown broadening outward as it retreats further into the picture plane (fig. 8). Hsü considered this the height of irrationality.

In real space, of course, it is a simple matter to determine the relationships between different objects, but how does one present

8 Ku K'ai-chih, Tsin dynasty:
Admonitions of the Court Instructress.
(detail)

three-dimensional objects on a two-dimensional surface? Oftentimes when looking at a landscape painting, we note how the middle and distant scenes are less defined and brightly colored than the foreground. This is referred to as atmospheric perspective and it is found in both Western and Chinese painting. Here, however, we refer to linear perspective, which pertains to the unfolding of a scene from a given viewpoint. Railroad tracks provide the classic example. Standing atop them, our eyes follow the two parallel lines into the distance, where they seem to converge, finally disappearing into a single point. This is a camera's view and it provided the model for painters in the West from the Renaissance until the nineteenth century. If we use this as a standard for perspective, then it is true that the Chinese approach appears somewhat wanting in logic.

In Chinese painting, three-dimensional objects are not always presented according to this principle of near-large, far-small. This is especially true with the painting of tables and smaller objects. A good example is found in "Court Ladies" (fig. 9) by an anonymous artist of the T'ang dynasty, in which we see that the table's width is actually broader in the back of the picture than in the front. More commonly in Chinese painting, an even distance is maintained from front to back. But is this form of expression truly irrational?

Three-dimensional space can only be suggested on a two-dimensional surface. The shapes of planes, for example, must be altered, as well as the angles between intersecting planes. When angles are altered, slanting lines are formed on the picture plane and these result in the illusion of space. Painting of architectural subjects in China, known as *chieh-hua*, or "lined painting," fully relies upon

slanting lines for creating the illusion of depth. The painter assumes an elevated prospect, looking slightly downward and sets his subjects along parallel slanting lines that recede into the distance. Insert 1 shows a schematic illustration of Western-style one-point perspective. As one finds in a photograph, the three-dimensional object follows the principle of near-large, distant-small, with the borders converging as one moves further into the picture. In Chinese lined painting, the borders of the object maintain an even distance as they recede in space; sometimes they even grow slightly apart (insert 2). In this manner, the visual integrity of the plane formed by these lines is fully preserved. There is no disappearing point of convergence. Depth continues to be suggested as long as the picture plane allows the parallel lines to develop.

It is not a question of which may be superior, the Western-style mode of portraying depth or the Chinese. Rather, we should recognize the salient characteristics of these two different modes of description. With one-point perspective there is an extremely strong sensation of depth, but with parallel slanting lines, the benefit is an opportunity to portray clearly objects in an unfolding scene. Some might criticize this approach as being overly simplistic, even child-like. However, consider the following point. If a craftsman were asked to fashion an exact copy of what is seen in Insert 1, he would wish to know whether the object portrayed is drawn in perspective or precisely according to its actual shape, with oblique angles and planes. There would be no such question with what is seen in Insert 2,

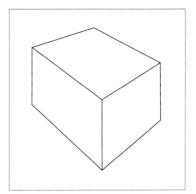

Insert **1** Cube.

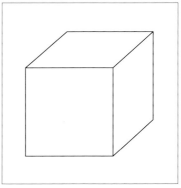

Insert **2** Cube.

which consequently allows us to conclude that this method of portrayal better preserves the true nature of a three-dimensional object. If the face of an object is portrayed in precise alignment with the picture plane, then there is no way that its sides can be shown. With the method adopted in Chinese painting, however, the representative frontal plane is presented fully, accompanied by the side and top. In comparison to Western one-point perspective, this method more closely approaches reality.

The principle of near-large, far-small has actually been known and practiced in Chinese painting since ancient times. This occasional willingness to ignore it is the result of the artist's intention to recreate the experience of his or her subject. The portrayal of space need not be limited to the fixed prospect as found in one-point perspective. The moving perspective utilized in Chinese painting is equally, if not more, effective, for it avoids the problem of foreground elements blocking the view of background objects and allows a clear presentation of both.

With the advent of modern painting, one-point perspective has lost its status as a fundamental standard. Looking at a diagrammatic sketch of a Picasso still-life (insert 3), we might ask what difference is there between this twentieth century master's handling of a table with what is seen in "Court Ladies" (fig. 9). Modern psychology has determined that human perception, unlike the lens of a camera, assigns a value of constancy to what is seen. As far as the optic nerve is concerned, the size and color of an object may appear differently as its position or angle is changed, yet a constant impression is maintained. The relative height of a telephone pole is still understood regardless of its distance from the viewer.

Many now recognize that the shifting perspective adopted in Chinese landscape painting more closely approximates the actual experience of landscape. Various scenes can be brought together, as the viewer is not limited to one fixed prospect. By the same token, with the viewer's prospect moving, the length or width of an object can remain the same whether it is in the foreground or background.

Certainly, a painting need not present nature precisely the way it appears in a photograph. It is only when the human factor is added that a painting attains true interest. A number of phenomena are born in paintings that seem to be contrary to science and how they are handled depends entirely on the painter. In Chinese painting one notes, in particular, the artists' application of such paired concepts as "emptiness and substance" and "unusual versus orthodox." These, which add to the richness of Chinese painting, will be addressed in the following chapter.

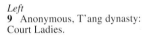

Left
9 Anonymous, T'ang dynasty: Court Ladies.

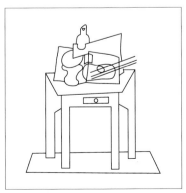

Insert **3** Picasso still-life.

Chapter Two
Paradise on Earth
Idea-realms in Landscape Painting

1. Ideas and Landscape

The application of the term *i-ching* (idea-realm) in the arts has its origins in literature. Wang Ch'ang-ling of the T'ang dynasty wrote of three realms in poetry: ideas, objects and feelings. The poet Chu Ch'eng-chüeh of the Ming dynasty took this a step further, writing that what is marvelous in poetry derives entirely from the process of synthesis that occurs between ideas (*i*) and scene (*ching*). In the early years of the Republican Period, Wang Kuo-wei directly adopted *i-ching* as a standard for critiquing literature. He wrote that inwardly poetry can express one's feelings while outwardly it has the capacity to affect others. "It all comes down to the two elements of ideas and scene. In the best writing, the two are thoroughly integrated. At a lesser level one surpasses the other. If either is lacking altogether, then it cannot be called literature." After Wang Kuo-wei, the term was soon applied to painting, where it is now given a primary role in discussions of quality and meaning.

"Where in the human world can such a place be found?" This, the theme of the last chapter, largely arises from the concept of "idea-realm." Painters before the T'ang dynasty mostly applied their talents to figure painting, and in figure painting, the criteria for excellence revolved around the ideas of "transmitting the spirit through form" and "breath-resonance generated by movement." For this reason, *i-ching* and related terms were not applied. During the T'ang and Sung dynasties, however, landscape painting began to flourish and, as described in the last chapter, the artist began to apply his thought to the process of recreating a world within his painting. As the great Northern Sung landscape artist Kuo Hsi wrote, "The painter should create according to an idea and the viewer always utilizes this idea to examine the landscape." Kuo Hsi wrote that the essential was to create a world in which one could travel, gaze, roam and reside. Moreover, he encouraged painters to draw inspiration from poetry so that one's own universe could be formed in one's heart. He wrote, "It is only after one is thoroughly familiar with nature's landscape and the heart calls out in response that one begins to move freely in creating one's own world." Kuo Hsi may have been the first person to touch upon ideas related to *i-ching*. In the Yüan dynasty, painters adopted a more subjective approach to landscape painting. Paintings such as Huang Kung-wang's "Dwelling in the Fu-ch'un Mountains" (figs. 17, 122) and Ni Tsan's "The Jung-hsi Studio" (figs. 11, 124) obviously do not invite the kind of photographic standards of realism we applied to Fan K'uan's masterpiece. Although one rarely sees the term *i-ching* in writings of this period, by the late Ming dynasty, Ta Chung-kuang (1623-92) was differentiating between "actual realms,"

10 Kuo Hsi, Sung dynasty: Early Spring.

"true realms" and "other-worldly realms" in his discussion of landscape painting.

In my opinion, while such factors as theme and technique help determine the nature of a painting's expressive potential, *i-ching* is the strength by which a painting in its entirety moves the viewer. Let us look briefly at the Northern Sung painter Hsü Tao-ning's "Evening Songs of the Fishermen" (figs. 14, 15). The flat expanse of a river scene unfolds before our eyes. In an imposing manner, high distant mountains rise and dip like ocean waves. River and streams flow naturally and realistically. As people of the Sung dynasty described, this is a painting in which one can travel, gaze, recline and roam. What marks the idea-realm of Hsü Tao-ning's work above all else is a naturalistic, concrete expression of space.

Now we turn to Kuo Hsi's painting "Early Spring" (figs. 10, 13). In front, grand pines grow from a great rounded boulder painted with the so-called "cloud-top" texturing effect (in imitation of the crowns of cumulus clouds). It is a technique that well captures the nature of the earthy mountain landscape of central China. The mountain peaks possess a delicate beauty, partly veiled by clouds and mist which impart a sense of ceaseless movement and change. Just as its title implies, the painting conveys to the viewer a sense of spring's awakening, that moment when winter finally recedes and life regenerates. The painting reveals Kuo Hsi's surpassing ability to model a landscape and infuse it with depth and atmosphere. As Kuo Hsi wrote, "Spring mountains are lightly adorned and seem to be smiling." Truly, one intuits this idea while looking at this painting. Earlier idea-realms, such as those seen in Fan K'uan's and Hsü Tao-ning's paintings, seem stern and objective. In comparison, Kuo Hsi's *i-ching* reveals the gradual merging of feeling with scene.

If the idea-realm is something sensed from beyond the painted scene, then there are a number of well-known works of the Southern Sung period that are characterized by a profoundly lyrical quality— a "poetry-realm." In many Southern Sung landscapes, the emphasis is placed on the foreground elements, and it is these that establish the painting's theme. It is as if a small piece of the world is cut away and presented for our study. Comparing the Southern Sung painter Mao I's "Swallows and Willow Trees" (fig. 12) with Hsü Tao-ning's "Evening Song of the Fishermen," we note that Mao I's fan uses a diagonal composition to assemble the large and small elements of his scene. The broad expanse of the distant area is left unpainted. Emptiness, here, takes the place of substance, providing the viewer with space for far-reaching thoughts. In poetry, it is often subtlety, circuitry and suggestion that are valued. Circuitry and suggestion are precisely the characteristics of poetic lines known to have been used to test academy painters at the Sung dynasty court, as the following two examples reveal:

Enveloped by bamboo by the side of a bridge, a rustic wine shop.

Remote waters—no one to ferry;
A lone boat gently rocks the entire day.

Wang Kuo-wei, as mentioned earlier, wrote that when idea and

11 Ni Tsan, Yüan dynasty: The Jung-hsi Studio.

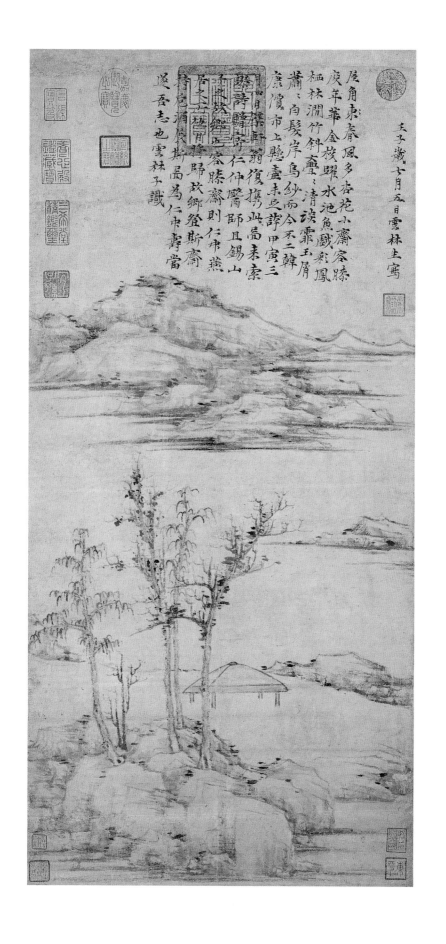

壬子歲七月五日雲林生寫

庭角東春風多杏花小齋容膝
庚年華金椒躍水池魚戲影鳳
栖林澗竹斜奄清谈霏玉屑
蕭然白髮岸紗而今不二韓
康賞市上懸盡未見許甲寅三
月授韓翁復携此屬來索
懸詩贈詩子仁仲醫師且錫山
不問故鄉谷膝齋則仁仲燕
居憩湎足歸故鄉登斯齋
遠吾志也雲林子識

scene are fully integrated, the finest results are produced; otherwise, one dominates at the expense of the other, or worse, one is absent altogether. Commonly, it is less a matter of scene or idea not being present as it is one being singled out for emphasis. This is especially true in landscape painting. We say that in general Sung landscape paintings sketch real scenery and Yüan landscapes sketch ideas. In other words, scene dominates idea in Sung; idea dominates scene in Yüan.

Let us regard some examples, beginning with Fan K'uan's "Travelers among Mountains and Streams." In this painting, which depicts the actual mountainous scenery of the Hua-shan region, the cliffs, slopes and towering mountains that fill the scroll all express strength and magnificence. Now we turn to Hsia Kuei's "Pure and Remote Views of Streams and Mountains" (fig. 16). The landscape in this painting is clear and spacious; the effect is bracing. This aesthetic effect is the idea-realm of Hsia Kuei's painting, formed from the assemblage of images in the painting's space. The painter's ideas and feelings merge with real scenes of landscape, but it is still the scene that dominates. Hsia Kuei's ideas are subtly hidden.

In Yüan dynasty landscape painting, there is a turn towards self-expression. Yüan artists again rely upon actual landscape for their forms and inspiration, but now it is ideas, perhaps even feelings, that forge the scenery. The title of Huang Kung-wang's "Dwelling in the Fu-ch'un Mountains" (figs. 17, 122) clearly states that the subject of his painting is this particular region of China between the provinces of Chekiang and Anhui, but there is little of that sense of verisimilitude that we note in the paintings of Sung artists. What we are drawn to is the refinement of Huang Kung-wang's brush and a sense of delight in its playful movements.

A Ch'ing dynasty critic named Huang Yüeh wrote of twenty-four categories of painting, following a model established for poetry by the T'ang critic Ssu-k'ung T'u. These present a very different picture from the four categories of ancient times: "divine," "untrammeled," "marvelous," and "capable." Now, as Huang Yüeh's categories reflect, paintings are all evaluated on the basis of idea-realms. Only "breath-resonance" (ch'i-yun), which stands somewhat apart from the others in this list, remains from the criteria used by ancient writers.

2. Transmitting the Spirit in Figure Painting

Landscape painting provides us with the illusion of another world here on earth. But what of the other subjects of Chinese painting: figures, flowers, birds and animals? Can these too be discussed and evaluated in terms of i-ching? I would say yes. In drama, emotions such as happiness, sadness and anger all must be conveyed through the particular skills of an actor or actress. Good theater draws the viewer in. It is the same for a good painter, who must be able to express the emotions of his figures, to lead the viewer into another world. As for the other subjects, the painter of these too can establish individual worlds in which ideas can be expressed. As the old saying goes, " A single flower, a single bird—a world within."

Long ago in the T'ang dynasty, the famous painter Wu Tao-tzu painted a Buddhist hell scene in the capital Ch'ang-an. His portrayal

Huang Yüeh's
Twenty-four Categories of Painting

 1. Breath-resonance
 2. Divine and Marvelous
 3. Lofty and Antique
 4. Hoary and Rich

 5. Steady and Forthright
 6. Penetrating and Calm
 7. Light and Distant
 8. Plain and Awkward

 9. Transcendent
10. Unusual and Novel
11. All-encompassing
12. Moist and Fluid

13. Barren and Frigid
14. Clear and Open
15. Personal and Soulful
16. Primordial and Unhewn

17. Mysterious and Deep
18. Bright and Unsullied
19. Vigorous and Upstanding
20. Simple and Concise

21. Refined and Conscientious
22. Handsome and Refreshing
23. Ethereal and Numinous
24. Beautiful and Gracious.

12 Mao I, Sung dynasty:
Swallows and Willow Trees.

Overleaf left
13 Kuo Hsi, Sung dynasty:
Early Spring (detail).

Overleaf right
14 Hsü Tao-ning, Sung dynasty:
Evening Songs of the Fishermen (detail).

15 Hsü Tao-ning, Sung dynasty: Evening Songs of the Fishermen.

16 Hsia Kuei, Sung dynasty: Pure and Remote Views of Mountains and Streams (detail).

17 Huang Kung-wang, Yüan dynasty: Dwelling in the Fu-ch'ung Mountains (detail).

Northern Sung landscape painting

Southern Sung landscape painting

Yüan landscape painting

fully conveyed the horrors and miseries of the underworld. Scurrying demons and monsters were fierce and frightening, while the tortured were shown wracked with suffering. Viewers of Wu Tao-tzu's painting felt as if they were living the scene themselves. It is said that meat butchers who saw it quit their killing professions, petrified by the sight of this possible retribution. Could a scene as effective as this not have possessed within it Wu Tao-tzu's ideas? Unfortunately, we cannot see for ourselves—Wu's paintings have long disappeared. We can, however, examine the drama of another painting, "Hsiao I Steals the Lan-t'ing Preface" (fig. 18), which was once ascribed to the T'ang painter Yen Li-pen. Seated on the antique chair is the Buddhist monk Pien-ts'ai, owner of the most famous work of Chinese calligraphy, Wang Hsi-chih's "Preface to the Poems Written at the Lan-t'ing (Orchid Pavilion)." Seated to the right, dressed in a white robe and hatted, is Hsiao I, who secretly possesses the order from the T'ang emperor T'ai-tsung to steal the Preface. Pien-ts'ai is portrayed as a wise, compassionate man of faith, with long eyebrows drooping downward to help express his sagacity. The palm of his left hand faces upward and his body inclines forward as he speaks. It is a position and manner that expresses Pien-ts'ai's openness—his willingness to reveal the fact that he is, indeed, in possession of the Orchid Pavilion Preface. In contrast, Hsiao I is portrayed as crafty and untrustworthy, with eyes looking slightly upward and lips tightly sealed. Most notable is the manner in which his two hands remain hidden deep within his sleeves, just as his motives remain hidden from view. The seated monk slightly behind and between Pien-ts'ai and Hsiao I appears unhappy, as if aware of what is about to transpire. The old and young attendants at the side preparing tea are oblivious to the unfolding drama, which, with its life-like portrayal of the figures, draws the viewer in deeply.

Figure painting has its own special aesthetic term: "transmitting the spirit" (*ch'uan-shen*). The term, in its basic definition, refers to the expression of an object's essence or spirit. It may suggest the successful portrayal of an actor's character, or the lifelike-ness of a realistic portrait. It may even suggest the perfect conveyance of an individual's habits and manners of speech and body. If the special

(detail: Buddhist monk Pien-ts'ai)

characteristics that define a subject are conveyed, the spirit is transmitted. *Ch'uan-shen* has come to be associated almost exclusively with figure painting and more specifically portraiture. In ancient times, it was figure painting that was considered the most difficult, and for a very simple reason: the accuracy of an individual's likeness was something that could easily be judged. On the other hand, the painting of things of the imagination, such as ghosts and demons, was considered comparatively easy, as no one could determine the accuracy of a picture of something never seen.

Form is the basis of painting, but it is those painters who go beyond form to express spirit that create the best work. A recorded story recounts how the two T'ang dynasty painters Han Kan and Chou Fang were both commissioned by a man named Chao Tsung to paint his portrait. Everyone who saw the two paintings thought they were both excellent, and as they were both by the hands of famous painters, Chao Tsung's father-in-law, Kuo Tzu-i, hung them together in his hallway to try and determine which was superior. In the end, however, he could not decide. Then one day Chao Tsung's wife returned home for a visit and Kuo Tzu-i asked his daughter if she recognized the subject of the portraits. "That's my husband," she answered. "And which painting is more accurate?" her father asked. She responded that both look very much like him, but one (referring to Chou Fang's) shows more than just outward appearance. It also captures his personality—his manner of speaking and smiling. Kuo Tzu-i's daughter was someone who understood painting and her answer reveals that Chou Fang was an artist who knew how to convey the essence that characterized his subject.

As an example of traditional Chinese portrait painting, we present the work of Shen Chou (1427-1509), the senior of the Four Great Masters of the Ming dynasty (fig. 19). The composition is pyramidal and frontal. Shen Chou's long white eyebrows and whiskers give him the appearance of a sage-immortal. His eyes are sharp and penetrating, his hands, with the exception of a single fingernail, remain hidden within his sleeves. Shen Chou's manner is steady, composed and gentle, but does it look like him? Directly above his head, Shen Chou added an inscription:

Some consider my eyes too small. Others find my jaw too narrow. I wouldn't know, nor would I know what might be lacking. What is the point of comparing eyes and face? My only fear is that "virtue" be lost. So negligent, these eighty years, and now death is barely a step away. (Dated) 1506. The Old Man of the Stone Field.

Looking at Shen Chou's portrait, we understand how some might consider Shen's eyes a bit small and his chin a bit narrow, but we also know from various sources that he was a learned, well-cultivated man, even of temperament and exceptionally broad-minded. Shen Chou lived all of his life in Suchou, where he gained remarkable status as a painter in the middle of the Ming dynasty and attracted numerous followers. This is a portrait that fully conveys Shen's cultured and virtuous manner. A year later Shen Chou inscribed his portrait again, this time to the side:

(detail: Hsiao I)

Left
18 Yen Li-pen, T'ang dynasty:
Hsiao I Steals the Lan-t'ing Preface.

Alike or not?
True or not?
A shadow on paper,
A person outside the body.
Life and death are a dream,
Heaven and earth of one dust.
Floating along life's stream,
I pass the years embracing my youth.

A sense of enlightenment emerges between the lines of Shen Chou's poem, and the viewer's admiration grows ever deeper.

The technical aspects of Shen Chou's portrait can be summarized in terms of brushwork and color. The painting is not physically large (71 x 53 cm) and thus posed no particular challenge. The clothing, too, is simple, comprised of quickly executed brushstrokes. More important, the painter utilized a thin "iron-wire" mode of linear description, with some modulation of thickness in the turns and angles (approaching a brush-mode known as "nail-head, mouse-tail"). In any case, the character of the brushwork is clean and concise. In comparison, the lines that describe Shen Chou's face are far gentler, pliant and fluid. From this we can see how different brush-modes impart different moods and impressions. The textures of Shen Chou's flesh and clothing also differ. For color, the artist used primarily ocher, to which was added a touch of vermilion in order to model Shen Chou's face and bone structure. Ink was added to ocher for the brown age spots; this adds to the character of the portrait. The technique is relatively simple, though it can be said that this enhances the forthright and honest character of the figure himself.

The small and interestingly composed handscroll in Figure 20 depicts Ni Tsan (1301-74), the famous painter of the Yüan dynasty. Ni Tsan sits comfortably on an elevated dais, his body draped in white robes. His right hand grasps a brush, supported by an armrest. His left hand holds a scroll of paper. In the screen behind Ni Tsan, a spacious landscape of mountains and lake is depicted. Ni Tsan was a high-minded scholar with lofty principles and is reputed to have been fastidious in matters of cleanliness. Not a speck of dust invades his image in the painting. His face, in particular, looks immaculate. Ni Tsan's neurosis about cleanliness is said to have been so strong that attendants had to sweep and clean wherever he went, and sure enough,

19 Anonymous, Ming dynasty:
Portrait of Shen Chou.

Left
20 Anonymous, Yüan dynasty:
Portrait of Ni Tsan
(with inscription by Chang Yü)

two such figures appear in the painting: a male attendant with a broom and a female holding a towel and basin of water. It is said that Ni Tsan once had a firmiana tree washed clean before he would recline in its shade. In another story, Ni Tsan ordered a water porter to bring forward only the bucket of water that he carried on a pole in front of him. Onlookers thought it strange that Ni Tsan would not use the second bucket that had been carried behind the porter, but Ni Tsan had his reasons: "Who's to say the fellow hasn't broken wind and polluted the back bucket? Would you drink such water?" Ni Tsan's portrait is unsigned, but it carries an inscription by Ni Tsan's contemporary, Chang Yü. Thus we know that the painting was done by someone of Ni Tsan's own time and one who was particularly keen to depict his subject's habits and personality.

Portrait painting is not simply a matter of likeness. The painter must proceed a step further and express his subject's mood and character. Traditionally in China, a painting would be praised according to the standard of "both form and spirit being complete," but is not spirit the more important of the two? The famous Tsin dynasty painter Ku K'ai-chih said if (surface) likeness is pursued too vigorously, the manner (and true likeness) will be lost. In the Ch'ing dynasty, Chiang I wrote in his "Secrets of Transmitting the Spirit," "Spirit resides in the eyes, feelings in the smile. Combining these two (spirit and feelings) will result in an excellent portrait." The face being the single most important component of a portrait, the painter must make a thorough study of how to handle it. Another treatise on figure painting, Wang I's "The Secrets of Portrait Painting" of the Yüan dynasty explains: "One discovers the true aspect of a person in their various manners of speech. One seeks this in absolute quietude. Silent understanding takes place in the heart so that even with eyes closed the subject seems right there and when the brush descends, the figure appears." In other words, it is only after careful investigation of a subject's appearance and manner that one might be able to duplicate Chou Fang's ability at capturing the exact manner of personality.

Before photography became wide-spread in China, painters had a lively business doing portraits. Today we commonly see their products in antique stores: images of ancestors dressed in their finery and rigidly posed in a formal manner. These are largely the work of little-known masters who operated at the local level. Interestingly, a portion of these reveal that body and costume were first carefully painted. The figure would remain headless until a suitable customer came along. Nowadays, all painters apply their talents to landscape, birds and flowers. Few people paint figures and even fewer use the traditional techniques of Chinese painting.

3. The Role of Emptiness and Substance in Composition

With regard to landscape painting, we have discussed the relationship between actual scenery and painting, the painter's process of internalizing and reconstituting the landscape and the expression of *i-ching*, "idea-realms." But how does the painter put these concepts into practice? The main ingredient is composition—the manner in which a painter constructs a landscape, just as a writer

21 Hsia Kuei, Ming dynasty: Gazing at the Waterfall.

constructs a poem or prose-piece. A painting, after all, is a painting, regardless of what is depicted, and at the purest level of appreciation, the first essential pertains to the manner in which a painter composes his forms and colors on the picture plane.

From Fan K'uan's "Travelers among Mountains and Streams," we have already learned something about composition and Chinese painting. Let us now look at a painting whose composition is somewhat simpler: "Viewing a Waterfall" by the Southern Sung painter Hsia Kuei (fig. 21). We absorb the painting's scene in a glance: a lakeside view of a small pavilion, some trees, a waterfall and the silhouette of distant mountains. However, there is complexity within the simplicity of Hsia Kuei's fan painting and many layers of subtlety. The transformation that has taken place from Fan K'uan's painting to Hsia Kuei's is indicative of the ceaseless effort Chinese painters applied to the art of composing their paintings. In landscape painting especially, one appreciates how a lone peak and solitary

Right above
22 Hsia Ch'ang, Ming dynasty: Small Window onto Lucid Green.

Right below
23 Ch'en Hsien-chang, Ming dynasty: Ten-thousand Flakes of Jade.

tree—just the small corner of a scene, as we find in "Viewing a Waterfall"—is still capable of expressing the idea of a limitless landscape that stretches on mile after mile.

In Chinese art, there are various phrases that refer to the preparation that takes place for painting, such as "the idea is present before the brush descends" and "the completed bamboo in the painter's heart." Both of these refer to a total grasp of one's subject before beginning to paint. There is another phrase, however, that more aptly describes what really takes place: "nine sketches, one completion." Nine simply means many, and what is translated as "sketch" refers to the charcoal-like material used for underdrawing in traditional China. The idea is that one can change and modify the sketches as many times as necessary and then, when one finally has it just right, the painting takes place. "Nine sketches, one completion" well describes the true process of painting, the necessity of revision and the efforts invested by traditional painters in the planning of their compositions.

That which draws the viewer into an excellent painting is its overall air and force (*ch'i-shih*) and this is determined by the disposition of the images and their various interrelationships. As an example, we look at the Ming dynasty artist Hsia Ch'ang's "Small Window onto Lucid Green" (fig. 22). Although only a single stalk of bamboo is depicted, stem and leaves are arranged with a sense of vibrancy and force. Ch'en Hsien-chang's "Ten-thousand Flakes of Jade" (fig. 23) similarly reveals the strength of a well-planned composition. In this case, a branch of flowering prunus unwinds from the upper right in graceful descent.

In the past, an important principle of Chinese painting was summarized by the saying, "To paint the hand plucking the five-stringed zither is easy, but to paint the eye sending off the flying geese is hard." The idea is that the eye can easily focus on a concrete action, such as the plucking of a string, but it is something else to convey the complex visual and emotional action that ties a subject's gaze to a bird at wing. Yet, if the *ch'i-shih*, energy or force, that ties the musician's gaze to the departing geese is not established, then the painting remains disjointed—the birds fly and the person plays, with no relationship created between them. An excellent demonstration of *ch'i-shih* is provided by the Yüan dynasty artist Chao Meng-fu's "Sheep and Goat" (fig. 24). Try to visualize this painting with all of the various collectors' seals and the Ch'ing emperor Ch'ien-lung's later inscription removed. The original composition is one sheep, one goat, Chao Meng-fu's inscription and signature in four lines at the left and his two seals directly following. The composition is exceedingly simple, yet it is enlivened by the subtle relationship established by the layout of the two animals. The plump, mottled sheep raises its head slightly and looks to its left. The mountain goat, placed slightly below, dips its head and looks to its right. The manner of the animals' two heads creates an unseen energy which is reinforced by their full postures. It is a circular, continuous energy not unlike the one seen in the well-known *t'ai-chi* diagram of *yin* and *yang* and it fully holds the viewer's interest.

In landscape painting, it is not simply the texture and weight expressed by brush and ink that determines a painting's excellence.

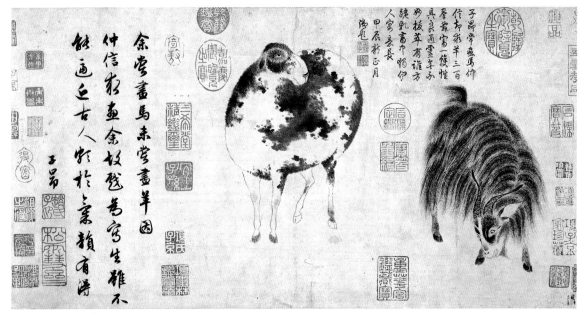

24 Chao Meng-fu, Yüan dynasty:
Sheep and Goat.

Another vital criterion is the composition's ability to establish
continuous lines of force integrating mountains, streams and forests,
for these lead the viewer into the scenery and guide one about the
scenery. "Assembled Green of Autumn Mountains" by the Yüan
dynasty artist Chu Shu-chung provides an excellent example (fig. 25).
Dominating the composition is an underlying zigzag design leading
down from the highest background peak. The viewer enters the
painting by the grove of trees at the lower right and is led smoothly
along arcing configurations to the distant heights of the landscape.

For the energies of *ch'i-shih* to appear, the artist must carefully
plan two sets of elements for his composition: "host and guest"
relationships and "void and substance." Host-guest relationships do
not exist among objects in actual scenery, but in painting they emerge
by necessity through the artist's decision to emphasize one element
over another. By definition, host and guest are related—one cannot
exist without the other. The Ming dynasty painter Kuo Hsü's "Hsieh
An and Courtesans" serves to illustrate this (fig. 26). Hsieh An's
formidable physical presence immediately establishes him as this
painting's host. His female companions, smaller and forming a
semi-circle behind, serve to highlight Hsieh An's central position.

"Emptiness and substance" is another way of describing the
concentration of ink and brushwork in a composition. In this regard,
it is precisely like the host-guest relationship: one is defined by the
presence or absence of the other. In landscape painting, all such
concrete phenomena as mountains, rocks, buildings, trees, bridges
and others are substantial. Water, air, mist and clouds, in contrast,
appear as insubstantial or "empty." The Ming artist Tai Chin's
"Riders Passing Over a Stream Bridge" (fig. 27) well illustrates
how substance and emptiness can be put to good use. His painting is
diagonally composed, with most of the painting's elements placed in
the triangle formed from upper left to lower right. The foreground
includes jumbled boulders in a fast-moving stream and a precipitous

bridge traversed by two riders and attending porters. The surface of the bridge and the water are empty; figures, horses, trees and rocks are substantial. In the middle-ground, a rocky precipice juts out over the water. To its right is the wide expanse of a placid river. A lone fisherman casts his line by the painting's right border. Water is empty; fishing skiff is substantial. In the middle-ground, emptiness begins to dominate while substance recedes. At the top of the painting, the higher the left-side peak rises, the broader the river's expanse and the more ground it occupies within the painting. All that is visible are two silent sailboats and distant hills rising and falling where water meets the sky. Top right and lower left divide into near-equal portions of emptiness and substance, but some empty spots exist in the dense substance of the foreground, while conversely, a few objects inhabit the emptiness of the distant background. The subtle interplay between the two is one of the marvelous qualities of this painting.

26 Kuo Hsü, Ming dynasty: Hsieh An and Courtesans.

Left below
25 Chu Shu-chung, Yüan dynasty: Assembled Green of Autumn Mountains.

Right
27 Tai Chin, Ming dynasty: Riders Passing over a Stream Bridge.

Chapter Three

The Art of the Line
Brushwork in Chinese Painting

1. Line and Brush

When color is removed from most Chinese paintings, one is left with an assortment of dots, assembled planes and lines possessing various degrees of modulation—all products of the painter's manipulation of the traditional Chinese brush. When we appreciate the brushwork in a given painting, our attention is drawn to these various lines, dots and textured surfaces. An excellent painter will utilize the description of form to express his or her feelings and ideas, and the brush is the means of conveyance. Lines can be thick or thin, rounded or sharp. The brush can move quickly to produce a sensation of fluid ease, or it can stutter fitfully, giving an impression of pent-up emotion. As it is in writing, painters have their own styles, or brush-tones. This is because personalities and techniques differ from painter to painter and such differences are conveyed to the viewer.

In the traditional critique of Chinese painting, two elements in particular are emphasized as fundamental: brush and ink. Brushwork, in fact, is such a noticeable component that Chinese painting has often been called a linear art, though the Chinese painter's and calligrapher's line should not be approached from the perspective of Western geometry. In Western painting, objects are described as an assemblage of surfaces rendered in shifting tonalities of light and shadow. This would seem to be beyond the capabilities of line alone, which in consequence may seem inadequate for describing the world's reality. Lines, however, can provide concise demarcations between areas of light and dark. Graduated tonal developments become unnecessary. There is a clarity here to the description of objects and this should be considered one of the merits of Chinese painting.

How exactly do dots and lines affect the viewer? The Ming artist Wen Cheng-ming's "Cymbidium and Bamboo" (fig. 28) is chosen to illustrate. The orchid leaves are described with lithe, sharp brushstrokes whose graceful character expresses the sensation of a wind-generated dance. Ignoring their descriptive function for the moment, we note that the strokes themselves are carefully modulated in thickness and beautifully curved. Looking at them, one almost feels one's own arms and legs stretching in answer. The single stalk of bamboo to the left of the orchid is formed section by section—pieces of straight lines rising upward. As for the bamboo leaves, the strongly modulated brushstrokes, with fat centers and tapered ends, are essentially straight lines as well. The painting is thus composed of the two most basic linear forms: the curved and the straight.

To demonstrate the aesthetic dimension of the line in Chinese landscape painting, we choose the Chin dynasty painter Wu Yüan-chih's "The Red Cliff" (fig. 29). Thin, sharp brushstrokes are used

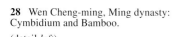

28 Wen Cheng-ming, Ming dynasty: Cymbidium and Bamboo.

(detail *left*)

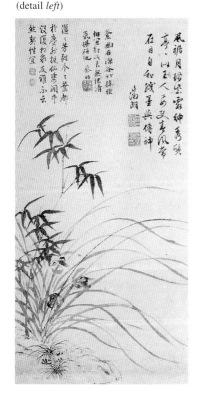

throughout the painting. Short strokes are used to elicit the hardness of the rocky cliff. Between the strokes, a percussive rhythm emerges in accompaniment to the rocking movements of the river's waves. One need not understand the content of the painting's story to be swept up into the very heart of the landscape by its skillful brushwork.

2. Methods of the Brush

"Use of the brush" (*yung-pi*) simply refers to the formation of dots and lines and for this, particular attention is paid to *pi-fa*, or "methods of the brush." Connoisseurs, in particular, savor each stroke of a painting and use this as the basis for discussing painting. Yet, paintings are composed of images, whose description, first and foremost, must be based on an object's appearance. The brush follows the forms of its subject and in this regard there can be no set methods. We can only speak in general terms of how brushstrokes are adjusted to unify a painting and express the ideas of the painter.

A number of specific terms related to brushwork have developed in China over centuries of practice. These include "reclining brush," "dragged brush," "broken brush," "trembling brush," "smooth brush" and "contrary brush."

"Reclining brush" describes brushwork rendered with the side of the brush. This is particularly seen in the texturing of surfaces in landscape painting.

The "dragged brush" refers to strokes formed with the belly of the brush dragging across the paper.

"Broken brush" is one whose tip has separated, usually from lack of ink, so that the surface of the paper is revealed within the brushstrokes.

With the "trembling brush," it appears as if the hand shakes while the brush stutters along and the line becomes alternately thick and thin.

The "smooth" and "contrary" brush-modes are both commonly seen. The former refers to an evenly paced stroke in which the brush-tip smoothly follows. The latter results from a reverse motion. With the smooth brush, the result is sharp, neat and graceful. With the contrary brush, the stroke staggers and possesses a pungent quality.

In the handling of the brush, a painter pays attention to "gathering and releasing," strength, speed, pauses, turns, modulations and folds. The viewer follows these qualities of the brush-line, as the eyes and feelings are stirred by the brush's expressive power. On the whole, the painter concentrates on moving and resting. Moving refers to continuous brushstrokes; resting refers to the pauses and stutters. When the former is emphasized, the brushwork floats with lightness and speed; when the latter dominates, the brush moves slowly and the effect is stiff.

3. The Description of Clothing Folds

The dress of traditional China featured wide robes and long sleeves, characteristics that proved extremely well-served by linear description in painting. Different methods in the handling of the brush would result in different effects. A detail from Ku K'ai-chih's "Admonitions of the Court Instructress" will demonstrate (fig. 30). The woman scribe's sleeves gently billow like scudding clouds. Her long skirt reaches to the ground. The outer appearance is soft and lingering, but this belies the tight, tensile internal structure. The brush is utilized very much as it is in the writing of the archaic seal script in

Above
29 Wu Yüan-chih, Chin dynasty: Red Cliff.

(detail *below*)

Chinese calligraphy: from beginning to end the brushstrokes are full, even and smooth. In ancient times, this brush-mode was described as "spring silkworms spitting silk." At first glance, there seems to be little to it, but the longer one looks, the more the subtle, circular movements build and carry the viewer. Ku K'ai-chih's brushwork begins in placid quiet, but by the end it is like charging winds and sheets of rain. Swirling robes are also a defining feature of an anonymous painting of a Buddhist divinity in the collection of the Shōsō-in Treasury of the Tōdai-ji Temple in Japan (fig. 31). The robes in this case are far less restrained. It was probably this kind of Buddhist image that gave rise to the description of one mural painting as "Heavenly clothing in swirling flight, a wall is filled with the force of a gale." Ku K'ai-chih's "Admonitions of the Court Instructress" expresses movement through subtle understatement. The Shōsō-in "Bodhisattva" conveys it directly and with unrestrained power.

The Ming dynasty critic Wang K'o-yü categorized the methods of painting clothing folds into eighteen types. Many of these are commonly seen, but some, such as the "olive pit" and "earthworm," are hardly ever used. In fact, it is often difficult to match paintings with the literary descriptions and labels that appear in early discussions. A considerable distance exists between words and images and how they are to be interpreted is likely to vary from one person to another. The examples offered here (fig. 32) have been chosen after consulting various sources and soliciting a range of opinions. In any case, the labels are a convenience and little more. The viewer should not be concerned with trying to attach them to what is seen in the paintings. The brushstrokes in Chinese painting are there to express precisely what the painter wishes to express. This is not something that could possibly be contained in eighteen categories.

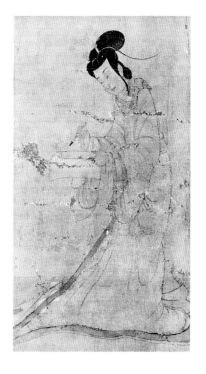

Above
30 Ku K'ai-chih, Tsin dynasty: Admonitions of the Court Instructress (detail).

Left
31 Anonymous, Nara period: Bodhisattva.

1. The Wandering Gossamer Stroke
of High Antiquity.
Associated with the description of clothing
folds in the tradition of the Wei painter Ts'ao
Pu-hsing. The strokes are sharply tapered.

2. The Zither String Stroke.
As one finds in the work of Chou Chü.

3. The Iron Wire Stroke.
As one finds in the work of Chang Wo.

4. The Moving-Clouds,
Flowing-Water Stroke.

5. The Locust Stroke.
As seen in the paintings of Ma Ho-chih and Ku Hsing-i. Also known as the Orchid Leaf Stroke.

6. The Nail-head, Rat's Tail Stroke.
Associated with the work of Wu Tung-ch'ing.

7. The Boat Prow Stroke.
Painted with a worn brush and associated with the paintings of Ma Yüan and Hsia Kuei.

8. Ts'ao's Robe Stroke.
The descriptive method of Ts'ao Pu-hsing.

9. The Folded Reed Stroke.
As one finds in Liang K'ai's painting, made of long, sharply tapered strokes.

10. The Olive Pit Stroke.
Associated with the painting of
Yen Hui.

11. The Date Pit Stroke.
Painted with a thick brush that
is sharply tapered.

12. The Willow Leaf Stroke.
Associated with Wu Tao-tzu's painting
of the Bodhisattva Kuan-yin.

13. The Trembling-brush, Water-ripples Stroke.

**14. The Bamboo Leaf
Stroke.**
Short strokes painted with the
belly of the brush.

15. The Earthworm Stroke.

16. The Bramble Brush Stroke.
Large, thick, abbreviated strokes.

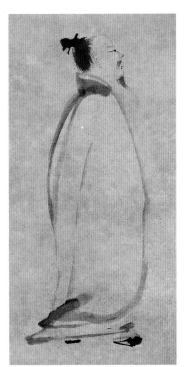

17. The Abbreviated Brush
Stroke.
As associated with Ma Yüan and Liang
K'ai.

18. The Mixed Brush Mode.

4. Texture Strokes in Landscape Painting

For brushwork in landscape painting, painters focus on texturing (*ts'un-fa*). The original meaning of *ts'un* is abrasion or scar. It is utilized here to describe surface patterns, commonly of rocks. The mountains of different geographical regions have their own unique characters. Cliff faces may surge and dip like ocean waves, or they may rise abruptly like giant swords. Some are rich with vegetation; others are hard and ungiving. To give shape to the various manners of landscape, the Chinese artist uses various brush techniques and lines. Different texture strokes express the artist's particular understanding of what he sees and wishes to express. Returning once again to Fan K'uan's "Travelers among Mountains and Streams" (fig. 6), we note that the surfaces of his boulders and mountain face are composed of thousands of short and middle-length "contrary strokes." The effect well conveys the impression of a mountain slowly worn by thousands of years of wind and rain. It also approximates the appearance of the mountains of northern Honan and southern Shansi, where Fan K'uan was active. This is called the rain-drop texture stroke. In contrast, the texture strokes seen in the Southern Sung painter Li T'ang's "Whispering Pines in the Gorges" (fig. 33) are formed with sweeping movements of an inclined brush that leaves triangular traces. These also suggest the hard mountains of the north, but of a different sort from those seen in Fan K'uan's painting. The rock faces of Li T'ang's painting appear to have been chiseled with the Creator's ax, an impression which has led to the label ax-cut texture stroke. Mi Fu's "Mountains and Pines in Spring" (fig. 34) presents the deep green mountains commonly seen in south China. Dot after dot is layered on the surface to suggest distantly seen trees moistened by rain and clouds. Mi Fu himself is credited with this descriptive technique—the Mi dot. Texturing methods are born from the artist's own careful study of nature. They are used to express the outlines of mountains, slopes and rocks, their concavities and convexities, the interplay of light and shadow and the record of geographic time as exhibited by their surfaces.

Over time, three different categories of texture strokes were developed pertaining to lines, surfaces and dots.

Linear texture strokes vary in length, such as the long and short hemp-fiber texture strokes. They also differ in their manner of turning, as one finds, for example, in the unraveling rope texture stroke, the lotus leaf texture stroke and the folding belt texture stroke. All of these are most suitable for describing soft, refined landscapes rich with vegetation and soil.

As for surface texture strokes, the large and small ax-cut strokes and the drag-through-mud-and-water stroke are most suitable for depicting steep cliffs and sheer angular rock faces.

Conglomerations of dot texturing, such as the rain-drop stroke and the Mi dot, are well suited for rendering grasses and trees half hidden by mist.

Texture strokes can produce radically different visual and emotional effects. Two examples from the previous chapter will demonstrate: Huang Kung-wang's "Dwelling in the Fu-ch'un

34 Mi Fu, Sung dynasty:
Mountains and Pines in Spring.

Mountains"(fig. 17) of the Yüan dynasty and Hsia Kuei's "Pure and Remote Views of Mountains and Streams" (fig. 16) of the Southern Sung. Huang Kung-wang's painting provides a classic demonstration of the hemp-fiber stroke. Within the soft, moist texturing is an overflowing sense of life. Hsia Kuei's painting relies upon ax-cut texturing. Rock faces are seemingly chiseled right out of the paper, their hard, solid textures as palpable as granite.

As it was with the linear brush-modes of clothing folds, texture strokes began as purely descriptive devices in accordance with the appearance of their subjects. It was the later critics who chose to emphasize their special characteristics and assign names. In time, they became models to study for those learning to paint, but they still cannot begin to summarize all of the complexities of a given landscape painting. To judge the quality of a painting on the basis of the recognizability of its brush and texture strokes would be the height of foolishness. In Figure 35, some of the more notable texture strokes seen in landscape painting are matched with details from paintings.

Left
33 Li T'ang, Sung dynasty:
Whispering Pines in the Gorges.

1. The Hemp-fiber Texture Stroke (long and short).
Soft strokes to suggest earthy hills. They modulate in tone for a graceful visual effect.

2. The Lotus Leaf Texture Stroke.
The brush-tip moves downward to create branching strokes suggestive of the veins of a lotus leaf. This mode is between the hemp-fiber and unraveling rope texture strokes.

3. The Roiling Clouds Texture Stroke.
Like floating pieces of clouds. Strokes are round and turning.

4. The Unraveling Rope Texture Stroke.
Related to the hemp-fiber texture stroke.

5. The Mi Dot.
The brush is inclined to one side to create olive-shaped dots which are varied in tone to suggest vegetation seen through a wet, misty atmosphere.

6. The Rain Dot.
Like a hail of rain assailing an earthen wall.

7. The Dot.
Similar to the rain dot, but round in shape.

8. The Demon-Face Texture Stroke.
Like skulls among the rocks, the stranger the better. Well-suited for the pitted rocks and coral of coastlines.

9. The Ox-tail Texture Stroke.
Painted with a fine brush. Dense strokes related to the short hemp-fiber stroke.

10. The Ax-cut Texture Stroke (large and small).

large   small

The brush is slanted and swept across to create triangular shapes.
Suitable for expressing hard rock surfaces.

11. The Folded Belt Texture Stroke.

Formed of smooth horizontal strokes with centered brush-tips.
The brush then angles downward into a slanting stroke.

12. The Horse-tooth Texture Stroke.

Repeated bald forms similar to a set of horse teeth. Suited to the description of sheer rock-faces.

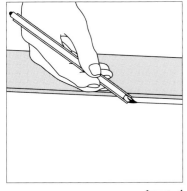

Insert **4**

5. Lined Painting

Clothing folds and rock texturing are all created from a free-moving brush. No implements are used to aid the painter's hand. However, a tool is used in the painting of architectural subjects—what is referred to as *chieh-hua* or "lined painting" (fig. 36). The meticulously straight lines that comprise the building seen in this detail of an anonymous Southern Sung painting were formed with the assistance of a ruler. The brush by itself cannot be used directly with a ruler. An open, tubular guide, upon which the brush rests, insures that the tip of the brush remains steady on the silk or paper and that the brush-line remains unmodulated (insert 4). It becomes easy to create lines of even width and length.

36 Anonymous, Sung dynasty: Entertainment in the Palace (detail).

Color Chart

	Mineral Pigments	Vegetable Pigments
Red	Ch'en-sha cinnabar (derived from mercury sulfide) Vermilion (darker than Ch'en-sha cinnabar, easily changes color) Red standard Tai ocher (from acidified iron) Yellow lead (minium)	Rouge (purple stem lac, cochineal, transparent red) Red Sandalwood (deep purple color)
Yellow	Mineral yellow (pure yellow) Yellow ocher Realgar, Red orpiment (from cockscomb stone; easily changes color)	Rattan yellow (gamboge; made from a clear yellow resin of the *hai-t'eng-shu* rattan) Gardenia yellow (a reddish yellow; made from gardenia seeds) Corktree bark, Chinese Scholar Tree flower
Blue	Mineral blue (ultramarine) Azurite (a form of mineral blue) Layered blue (a form of mineral blue, sky blue color) Light blue (a form of mineral blue) Granulated blue (Hui blue, Moslem blue, Tibetan blue)	Indigo, Flower blue
Green	Malachite (blue-green, turquoise) Copper green (man-made; easily changes color) Granulated green (slightly darker)	
White	White powder (white chalk, calcium carbonate; for mural painting) Lead white (ceruse) Foreign white, Tartar white (clamshell white)	
Black	Graphite (black paste, cosmetic black; used for description of fine hair)	Soot (for description of fine hair) Hundred-grass frost, Five-leaf alcibia ash

Common Color Combinations and their Uses

Name	Combination	Uses
Snail-shell blue	7 parts indigo + 3 parts light ink	Clothing, pine needles, *chieh*-character leaf motifs, pepper dots, shallow water, distant mountains, distant trees.
Leaf green	5 parts rattan yellow + 5 parts indigo	Spring trees, willow dots, summer leaves, bamboo, water plants.
Grass color	Leaf green with light ocher	Thatched huts, leaves, bamboo fences.
Ocher and ink	7 parts ocher + 3 parts light ink	Mountains and rocks in summer scenes, bridges, boats.
Light ocher and ink	8 parts ocher + 2 parts light ink	Autumn mountains and slopes, various leaves and tree trunks and branches, buildings and architectural features.
Rattan yellow and ink	6 parts rattan yellow + 4 parts light ink	Mountains and rocks of spring scenes, spring foliage.
Ocher yellow	8 parts ocher + 2 parts rattan yellow	Spring mountains.
Indigo		Distant mountains, buildings, clothing, water waves.
Ocher		Same as light ocher and ink, clothing.
Rattan yellow		Sometimes used for clothing.

Chapter Four

Polychrome Painting
Pigments and Color

Another name for painting in Chinese is *tan-ch'ing*, "the reds and blues." Red and blue are among the most eye-catching of colors and it is for this reason that they have come to represent polychrome painting in general. Most people think that Chinese painting emphasizes ink and that color plays a much diminished role. It is even said that the challenge of applying colors cannot compare with that of spreading the ink. This, however, is not an entirely accurate perception. If one considers the entire history of Chinese painting, then there is no avoiding the fact that the world through the T'ang dynasty was essentially multi-hued. Archaeological discoveries in this century have confirmed this. Moreover, the fourth of Hsieh Ho's Six Laws of Painting, which emerged in the sixth century, speaks directly of the importance of color: "application of colors according to kind." Nowhere in Hsieh Ho's laws is ink mentioned. Ink painting only began to gain currency in the middle of the T'ang dynasty with the emergence of Wang Wei (701-66) and other painters of his time. With the later rise of literati painting, ink painting gained popularity, eventually earning its place as the dominant feature in Chinese painting.

1. The Pigments of Chinese Painting

We begin with a discussion of the pigments, for understanding their character and effects will help reveal the particular characteristics of Chinese polychrome painting. Thousands of years of practice have revealed two basic categories of pigments: mineral and vegetable. Those most commonly used and their applications are presented on the opposite page.

The various combinations of colors outlined in the accompanying chart are the result of the shared experiences of painters over time. In China, one does not find the systematic study of colors that exists in the West, and there are no absolute standards for colors. Nor is there much quality control—a single color produced by one manufacturer over time may well alter in density of tone and brightness. Nonetheless, the colors described here are fairly standard and common. One point that is important to note is that mineral pigments, in general, are more stable than vegetable pigments. As long as a painting is properly preserved, mineral pigments will not change in appearance over a long period of time. Vegetable pigments, on the other hand, are prone to fading. If not well kept, vegetable pigments tend to turn black or yellow in tone, or fade away altogether. Another important point is that mineral pigments are not by themselves adhesive. A binding medium is necessary. Usually alum is added to keep the colors from spreading.

37 Ma Lin, Sung dynasty:
Night Outing with Candles.

2. Colors and Light

Chinese painters seek the intrinsic color of the subject, not its momentary appearance under some particular condition of lighting. This is already revealed in Hsieh Ho's dictum that the application of colors is in accordance to kind. Kind refers to the subject's general category or class—that which is unchanging. In the painting of a red flower vase, the Western artist may use a bit of white pigment to show the light's reflection off the vase's surface. Various tones of red, as well as other colors, are used to suggest the rest of the vase. In contrast, the Chinese painter will use a pure, uniform red pigment for the entire vase.

Following the principle of applying colors according to kind, color can be considered one of the factors that expresses a subject's spirit. For this reason, it is not the appearance of the color that is important but the subject's eternal, unchanging nature. Taking mountains as an example, Kuo Hsi wrote, "Spring mountains are lightly adorned and seem to be smiling. Summer mountains are richly green, dripping with moisture. Autumn mountains are bright and lucid, well-attired. Winter mountains are cold and desolate, as if asleep." As for water: "Spring water is green, summer water jade-green, autumn water is blue and winter's is black." And the sky: "Dazzling in spring, brilliant blue in summer, clear in autumn and dark in winter."

Light has a decided effect on colors. Let us take a look at how Chinese painters chose to handle night scenes. In Western painting, colors appear wherever light illuminates the darkened setting, much as one sees in reality. Chinese painters, however, adopt a different approach. In fact, in Chinese painting, little difference is apparent between night and day scenes. Rather than darken the setting, the Chinese painter will use certain signs to indicate it is evening—lanterns, candles lit along a terrace, a glowing moon, or the lake mists associated with the lateness of day. The Southern Sung painter Ma Lin's "Night Outing with Candles" will serve as an example (fig. 37). In a six-sided pavilion, a gentleman sits in repose. A bright moon shines in the clear sky. Facing the entrance are four pairs of tall candles lining the walkway. Flowering crab apple trees spread their branches in the even moonlight. The night air hangs heavy, but the suggestion is exceedingly subtle: just the glow of interior lights under the pavilion's eaves to impart a sense of the night's darkness. Such soft beauty could not be expressed with color alone.

In contrast to Western painting's utilization of a fixed light source, one finds in Chinese painting a fluid interplay between light and dark (*yin* and *yang*), with no single source of illumination. This approach, which may at first seem to reflect a lack of understanding of physical properties, highlights the Chinese painter's emphasis of movement, vitality and spirit. The Ch'ing dynasty painter Kung Hsien (1619-89) wrote:

When painting rocks, one makes their tops white and their bottoms black. The white is *yang* (bright); the black is *yin* (dark). Most of a rock's surfaces are flat, hence they are white. Those that face upwards and catch the light of sun or moon are always rendered white. The sides of rocks are often cracked or covered by moss and grasses; otherwise they face downward, shaded from sun and moon. Hence they are black.

As for the application of colors, the Ch'ing dynasty painter T'ang I-fen (1778-1853) commented:

There are many methods of coloring. In each case one must consider what is suitable. In some cases, colors are applied to the dark (yin) parts of a painting, leaving the bright (yang) parts in reserve. Other times colors are used for the bright passages while ink alone is used for the dark. Sometimes the bright and dark portions are created solely from ocher with the dotting done in blue-green. Other times bright and

38 Yun Shou-p'ing, Ch'ing dynasty: Autumn Flowers (detail).

dark are rendered purely with blue-green accompanied by ink-wash. Sometimes the bright is described with ocher while the dark relies on ink mixed with blue. Other times the bright is created from blue while the dark is made from ink mixed with ocher. Sometimes ocher is used only for small rocks and oblique slopes; sometimes it is used only for texturing. Sometimes ocher is used only for human faces and tree trunks. Blue and green can be used solely for the dotting of moss and leaves. It can also be used solely as a wash for sky and water.

3. Harmonizing Colors

While there may be different methods of color application, our reactions to them are fundamentally the same. Warm colors like red and orange stir our feelings while cool colors like blue and green impart a sensation of bracing calm. It is said that the Five Dynasties Period ruler Liang Yüan-ti authored an essay titled "Standards of Pines, Rocks, Mountains and Water." He wrote, "Flaming red, cold green, the warmth of the sun, the chill of the stars." This is in reference to pure unadulterated colors. The combining of pigments can produce more complex results. It all depends on the painter's skill.

Combining pigments is the most difficult part of applying colors. In a text titled *Hua shuo* attributed to the Five Dynasties Period painter Ching Hao, it is written, "A bit of yellow in the red, autumn leaves fall. Green within the red, flowers flourish. Purple within blue and it will not seem dead. A touch of yellow in the white to add a glow." And Tsou I-kuei (1686-1772) of the Ch'ing dynasty wrote, "Blue and indigo do not go well together, nor can white and yellow follow one another. Brilliant red and purple can be used once or twice, but the results will be unusual if you combine deep and light shades of green." As any experienced artist knows, adjusting the tonal balance of one color is not difficult, but when a number of different colors are combined, one must be dominant while the others play a subordinate role. The principle here is more or less the same for both Western and Chinese painting. "Cold and warm, strong and weak, large and small, light and dark—these are all things determined by tones of color. An excellent artist will understand the subtleties of utilizing color tones." Tsou I-kuei once again reminds us that all artists must pay close attention to color harmony. As a good example, we present a leaf from an album by Yun Shou-p'ing (fig. 38). The choice and application of colors in this scene of autumn flowers is superb. The effect is at once gorgeous and refined.

In traditional Chinese painting, there is a type of painting that utilizes strong, heavy colors. Their application tends to be neat and orderly and the overall effect is sumptuous. For landscape painting, it is commonly referred by the labels "gold and green" and "green and blue." The dazzling quality of the former is easily imagined. For the latter, mineral pigments are used to express a sense of nature's overflowing abundance. Gold is the most eye-catching of colors. In landscape painting, it is particularly suited for depicting the brilliance of a sunlit scene. The Sung painter Li T'ang's "Small Scene of Rivers and Mountains" illustrates this point (fig. 39). Small touches of gold pigment are applied to the rocks of the cliff and along the bank to suggest the reflection of sunlight on a brilliant summer day. This effect is subtle but essential, just like the painting of the pupils of the eyes to bring the dragon to life, as an old story goes. Similarly, gold paint is sometimes used to highlight peonies. Red, purple and even ink peonies all present an air of lofty transcendence when the flower stamens and leaf veins are touched with gold. There is another kind of painting which appears on gold foil paper. This format was especially popular for fan paintings during the Ming dynasty. When colors are applied to this kind of surface, the effect is rich and decorative. The example chosen here is a Southern Sung painting of quails (fig. 40). White pigment combines with the gold ground to bring out with sparkling effect the patterning of the birds' plumage.

39 Li T'ang, Sung dynasty: Small Scene of Rivers and Mountains.

40 Anonymous, Sung dynasty: Quails.

Blue-green landscapes are referred to as "greater" or "lesser" depending on how heavily the mineral pigments are applied. The process itself is rather complicated. Commonly, it is the upper portions of mountains and rocks that receive the thickest applications of pigment, with the tone gradually lightening towards the bottom. In general, ocher is first used as a wash for the lower portions of rocks and mountains. Ink-darkened blue and a warm green are applied as base colors on mountain slopes. Then layer after layer of mineral blue and malachite are added. The process is called "three-alum, nine-wash" because after every one or two applications of color, a transparent binder made with alum must be applied to stabilize the colors and keep the various layers of washes from becoming muddled. Only after the repetitive process bestows a feeling of substance to the painting is it considered finished. Tree foliage is usually depicted in ink outlines, with colors then filling the interiors (chosen in accordance with the season). If the painting is a "lesser" blue-green landscape, then the colors are harmonized with extensive use of inkwash. In contrast with the thick heaviness of the "greater" blue-green, the impression is light and supple. "Festival in the Provinces" (fig. 41), attributed to the tenth century painter Tung Yüan, can be used as an illustration of the blue-green landscape. As the detail reveals, ocher pigment was used as a base color, which becomes rocks and earth where left uncovered. Mineral blue and green pigments are overlaid to create grassy slopes. This is a classic example of the "greater" blue-green style of landscape painting.

Right above
41 Tung Yüan, Five dynasties period: Festival in the Provinces.

(detail *right below*)

Below
42 Chao Ch'ang, Sung dynasty: New Year Flowers.

Flowers and birds epitomize the richness of color. In fact there are many who believe that the primary function of bird-and-flower painting is to show off the beauty of the colors. If there is an equivalent of the heavily colored landscape in bird-and-flower painting, then it would have to be represented by the palace-style flower painting of the Sung dynasty, of which Chao Ch'ang's "New Year Flowers" (fig. 42) is a good example. Narcissus, camellias and peonies fill the surface of the silk with uncommonly thick colors. A mineral blue pigment was added to fill in the background. This assists in highlighting the beauty and vivacity of the flowers. An ornamental Lake T'ai-hu rock completes the small scene, which suggests a wealthy aristocrat's early spring garden.

There is another kind of polychromatic painting called the "boneless style." This consists of pure colors and no outlining in ink. Yün Shou-p'ing's album leaf of autumn flowers is an excellent example (fig. 38). In this manner of painting, the movements of the brush can still be discerned. The colors are not too heavy, so the impression is one of untamed elegance. There is also a boneless style of landscape.

43 Emperor Hui-tsung, Sung dynasty: Beating the Silk.

Heavy applications of color can also be seen in figure painting. As an example, we use the Sung dynasty emperor Hui-tsung's copy of "Beating the Silk" by the T'ang dynasty painter Chang Hsüan (fig. 43). The palace women are depicted in the midst of their labors, yet they still maintain an air of aristocratic beauty. This is in part due to the artist's description of their forms and bearing, but it also arises from the painting's rich application of colors. The coloring of their silk garments is superb and even more so is the subtle harmonies they create as a group. Malachite and azure long skirts are combined and contrasted with brilliant reds and pink. White pigment is added and subtle patterning is rendered on the women's garments to emphasize variation within the colors and to help unify the ensemble.

Chinese artists like to use this method of contrasting colors in their paintings. Another example by Yun Shou-p'ing is chosen to illustrate. Here, the red of the flowering peony is boldly juxtaposed with green foliage (fig. 44). The goal of contrasting colors is to awaken the eye without creating dissonance. The method depends on the suitability of color combinations, but it is also important to recognize the fine and delicate nature of Chinese pigments and the painter's habit of incorporating unpainted areas into his or her composition. These factors broaden the possibilities of the artist's assemblage of colors. For color washes, the artist mixes pigments with water to create various tones of transparent color. In the lesser blue-green style, for example, light washes of malachite and blue combine with the natural ground for lively effect.

There are no fixed rules for the application of colors, nor can all of the possible permutations of color be easily summarized by a few concrete principles. Heavily or lightly applied, colors can be used with captivating effect. What is important is that they harmonize within a painting and maintain a degree of elegance.

44 Yun Shou-p'ing, Ch'ing dynasty:
Peonies.

Chapter Five

The Spirit of Ink

Expressing the Resonance of Ink

1. Ink and Its Use in Painting

Form and color may be the basic components of both Western and Chinese painting, but their manners of expression differ greatly. Little attention is paid to lighting in Chinese painting, while black, white and the tonal shades in between play a particularly important role. As we all know, this black-and-white art is produced with ink. The mastery of ink joins that of the brush in forming the two fundamental criteria by which the performance of a painting is often judged.

Ink is made by mixing soot with glue, which is then formed into a cake or slab. The soot can come from various sources, including pine, oil or lacquer. When the slab is rubbed on an abrasive surface with water, black ink results. Ink possesses a number of special characteristics. Firstly, it is less susceptible to fading than pigments. A two thousand year old cloth painting of a female shaman dating from the Warring States Period confirms this: while the colors on the painting have almost entirely faded away, the ink traces remain perfectly clear (fig. 89). Similarly, Han dynasty writing on bamboo strips can still easily be read. Secondly, regardless of the material—wood, paper or silk—decomposition does not take place where the ink was applied. Most interestingly, once ink is made and dried, no matter whether it is a hardened pool or a single light line applied to paper or silk, it remains remarkably durable. Even if water is reapplied, it will not revert to liquid state. This is extremely important for painting, for it means that numerous layers of ink can be applied without fear of their running together. Moreover, this allows the paintings to be remounted, a process that involves immersion in water. Ink can be ground to a state of lacquer-like viscosity, or it can be made as light as filmy water. It can be used for writing or for painting. Being so versatile, it is little wonder that ink is so widely appreciated in China.

The use of ink in Chinese painting underwent one important transformation. This took place in the T'ang dynasty around the time of Wang Wei, when ink's flexibility and full potential began to be realized. Ink painting began to flourish and, in general, Chinese painting took a large step towards simplification. Before this, painting was a world of colors. Hsieh Ho wrote of the application of colors in accordance with kind and he wrote of the brush's role in structuring form, but he never mentions ink. It is not until the late T'ang and the art historian Chang Yen-yüan, writing in the ninth century, that ink is formally brought into the discussion of painting. "Wield the ink," he writes, "and the five colors will be realized." Black ink can bring out the layers of a scene. It can differentiate light from

45 Pa-ta shan-jen, Ch'ing dynasty: Lotus (detail).

dark, warmth from cold. It can describe mist, snow, rain and haze. The one drives the many; the complex is eschewed for the pure and simple. Ink can be broken down into six "colors," which refer to the qualities of appearing dry, wet, thick, light, black and white. Of course, a full tonal range is possible with ink. "Five" colors or "six" colors— these terms merely signify the unlimited flexibility of ink.

2. The Colors of Ink

In evaluating an artist's skill in using ink, one looks at the "colors" of his ink as they appear in a painting. There is an ancient description in China: "Masterly use of ink appears green; the lesser brush produces ocher." In my own opinion, it is not simply the color of the ink that impresses in a well-done painting, but something that captures the eye and makes the spirit soar. For an illustration, let us look at a detail of grapes from a scroll of fruits and flowers by the Ming dynasty artist Hsü Wei (fig. 46). Representation is not the primary issue—we are not so concerned with specifying what is what in Hsü Wei's painting. Rather, would it not be more appropriate to think of this as the image of beginnings, when form first emerges from primordial chaos? With its interplay of black and white, light and dark and wet and dry, Hsü Wei's *tour de force* can be appreciated as a work of abstraction. Another superb demonstration of ink is found in Pa-ta shan-jen's album leaf of a blossoming lotus (fig. 45). The composition is simple but novel, and the various layers of ink are rich in transformations. Each application of ink is perfectly clear to the viewer, yet the overall effect is unified: a lush image of dripping green. Pigments could hardly convey any better the lotus' sense of purity and coolness. Another example is provided by Chao Meng-fu's "Goat and Sheep" (figs. 24, 47). The woolly texture of the sheep's coat contrasts markedly with the long, needle-like hairs of the goat. This successful rendering of different textures largely stems from Chao Meng-fu's mastery of ink. He used soft wet tones to dot the mottled fleece of the sheep and a dry ink to describe the goat's stringy coat.

In the application of ink, it is not how varied the effects are that is important but how appropriate. The painter wants the viewer to sense the richness of the ink, its luminosity. An example of a relatively simple use of ink is a fan painting of bamboo by the Ming dynasty artist T'ang Yin (fig. 48). Dark and light tonal values separate the front leaves from the back. For an example demonstrating the complex use of ink, we turn to "A Thousand Cliffs and Myriad Ravines" (fig. 49) by the Nanking-based Ch'ing dynasty painter Kung Hsien. In this relatively small painting of album-leaf size, the landscape practically fills every square inch. Kung Hsien described painting as a matter of layering ink. Its application creates the tone of a dream journey through a vast, surrealistic universe. There is unlikely to be a better illustration of the subtle power of ink to carry the viewer into another world.

It should be pointed out that the beauty of ink largely depends on skillful brushwork. The two are inseparable: the brush relies on the ink to leave a trace and ink depends on the brush to reveal its expressive potential. As the saying goes, "The brush sings and the ink dances." The Southern Sung painter Liang K'ai's "Inkwash Painted

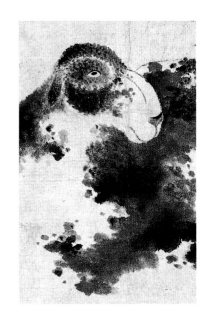

46 Hsü Wei, Ming dynasty:
Grapes (detail from a scroll of fruits and
flowers).

Left and below
47 Chao Meng-fu, Yüan dynasty:
Sheep and Goat (details).

Immortal" (fig. 51) confirms this. The strolling figure is exceedingly
strange, with belly exposed and facial features knit together under an
enormous brow. We note how the painter's tonal range varies in
density from the sheer black of the immortal's belt, approaching the
"scorched" quality of super-saturated ink, to the blank ground of
paper revealed in the figure's forehead, belly and chest. The "white"
of his body is brought out by the sleeves to either side. The artist's
handling of a wet brush soaked with ink is seen most clearly in the
broad sleeve that descends from the figure's right shoulder. To elicit
this effect, the entire brush was first immersed in light ink and then
the tip was tinged with a darker ink. The dark ink first touches the
paper as the brush moves downward. Lighter tones follow in five or
six strokes, imparting a soaring effect to convey the sage's forceful
gait. Brush and ink together reveal the artist's conception of uplifting
spirit as he sketched this unrestrained immortal.

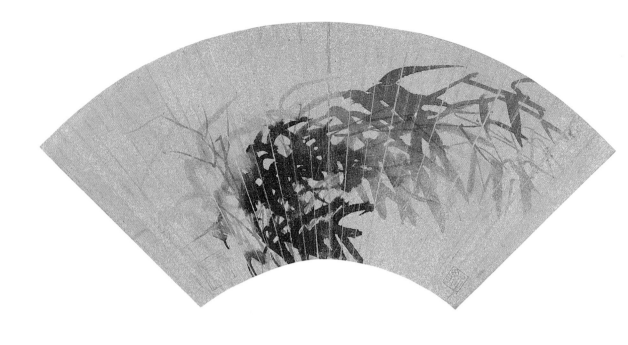

Monochrome ink painting by itself forms an important category of Chinese painting, but more common is a combination of ink with pigments. Thus, the painter must be thinking about how these two elements will act together in his painting. The general principle is that the two must be mutually supportive. There is an old saying that when neither hinders the other, then the ink will appear in the colors and colors in the ink. This idea can be said to conform with the chromatic principle that all colors can be adjusted in tone by adding varying shades of gray, all of which are easily produced by ink.

In general, a Chinese painting will be initiated with outlines described in ink. For figure painting, this corresponds to the descriptive lines of clothing and body; for landscape, it would be trees and rocks. In this manner, ink commonly provides the "bone structure" of the painting. Ink washes of light tone can then be added to complete the underlying structure. Colors are then applied and their luminosity and density tempered by the monochrome ink wash upon which they are laid. Adjusting the tone becomes a relatively simple matter. The colors can then appear light and transcendent while remaining rooted, or rich and seductive without appearing gaudy. In the application of colors to landscape painting, mineral blue and ocher are used most often. In places, these will be adjusted in tone by underlying layers of light inkwash to create secondary colors differing in density and brightness. Chromatic shifts can thus be gradual and harmonious, the gray tones of inkwash helping to establish buffer zones between what may begin as entirely different colors.

One form of flower painting that has developed in China is called "red-flower ink-leaf," and it is exemplified by the great master of recent times, Ch'i Pai-shih (1863-1957) (fig. 50). The red flower in this painting of a lotus is colored with a brilliant carmine while the leaves and stems are described in varying tones of ink. Red is the most excitable of colors; black settles the spirit. One lively, one subdued—somehow the atmosphere of the painting remains calm and right. At the same time, the opposition of red pigment and black ink allows each to express its own particular beauty.

Left above
48 T'ang Yin, Ming dynasty: Bamboo.

Left below
49 Kung Hsien, Ch'ing dynasty: A Thousand Cliffs and Myriad Ravines.

Right
50 Ch'i Pai-shih, 20th century: Lotus.

世行不
徹名和不
臘大以
高陽一
酒徒座
毫隱壺
仙宴罷
淋漓襟
袖尚糢
糊夢闊

3. Methods of the Ink

Ink, like the descriptive brushline and texture stroke, has undergone centuries of experimentation and collective experience to lead to the codification of a number of techniques used in painting. A few are briefly introduced here:

The "splattered ink" method, as the name implies, utilizes considerable quantities of ink that are practically poured onto the painting surface. In the T'ang dynasty, the painter Wang Hsia is said to have been wild of spirit and exceedingly fond of alcohol. Drunk, he would attack paper or silk with a wild splashing of ink. Then, chanting ditties, he would smear the ink with hand and foot, quickly shaping the chance configurations into images of mountains, rocks, clouds and water, so that by the time he was done, there was no suggestion of the ink's original stain (see Chapter 9.4). This description of Wang Hsia's invention of the "splattered ink" technique suggests something rather removed from Liang K'ai's "Inkwash Painted Immortal" (fig. 51), which clearly reveals the movements of the painter's brush. Nonetheless, the label has come, through common practice, to refer to a technique in which ink is applied both liberally and freely, with little sense of restraint to the wet pools and patches that result. Although the "splattered ink" technique appeared at least as early as the T'ang dynasty, very few examples exist that can be matched with the description of Wang Hsia's style. Hsü Wei's work (fig. 46), though of much later date, perhaps comes closest in spirit and technique.

Another ink technique is called "broken ink." The effect of ink first splattering the painting's surface is sometimes likened to the primordial state of undifferentiated chaos. At this time, different tones of graded ink must be used to add definition, allowing borders to be settled and forms to emerge. The initial dark mass is "broken" so that a new world can appear. In painting practice, this is really a matter of adornment. A simple example is provided by the belt on Liang K'ai's "Inkwash Painted Immortal." One jet black stroke girds his belly, two more sweep downward helping to define the striding sage's legs. All three are applied atop the paler area of wash that roughly marks his lower body.

The "piled ink" technique, as the name implies, consists of the layering of different shades of ink until the desired tonal value is reached. Painters in general are attracted to this particular method, for it allows one to feel the substance of the image as it is drawn out from the surface. In my opinion, Kung Hsien's "A Thousand Cliffs and Myriad Ravines" (fig. 49) presents the finest model for this technique.

51 Liang K'ai, Sung dynasty: Inkwash Painted Immortal.

Chapter Six
Common Roots for Writing and Pictures
The Relationship between Painting and Calligraphy

Some divide the arts into the eight major media: literature, theater, architecture, sculpture, painting, dance, music and cinema. Missing from this list is calligraphy, which, although one of the great arts in China, does not assume the same role of importance in Western society. In China, discussions of painting almost always touch upon calligraphy as well. The two arts are considered inseparable, like twins from birth. Formats and tools are fundamentally the same—brush, ink, paper and silk—and the basic manner in which the brush is handled. In traditional China, all educated people learned how to use the brush to write. For those whose interest turned to painting, it was only a matter of time before the habits and methods learned from calligraphy were transferred to painting.

Already in the ninth century, the T'ang dynasty art historian Chang Yen-yüan wrote that calligraphy and painting were two arts differently named but of a single origin. For examples he offered pictographic characters, whose forms still retain the images of what the characters represent. Chang Yen-yüan also touched upon the related use of the brush in both arts. We need not repeat what has already been mentioned in previous chapters, but it should be pointed out that the diversity that characterizes brushwork in painting is also found in calligraphy. This is best demonstrated with the character *yung*, "eternal," which is composed of eight different types of strokes when written in the standard script:

Eight types of strokes

ts'e (the dot),
le (the horizontal stroke),
nu (the vertical stroke),
yüeh (the bottom hook),
ts'e (the rightward inclined stroke),
lüeh (the long leftward descending stroke),
chuo (the short leftward descending stroke),
che (the rightward descending stroke).

The brush is handled differently for each of these calligraphy strokes. It is also used differently for different scripts. In the seal script, for example, strokes are rounded and have uniform thickness. In the clerical script, a single stroke can be highly modulated from thin to thick. In the cursive script, the brush may connect strokes and characters in a single fluctuating line. All of this depends on the calligrapher and how he or she personally handles the brush. In summary, calligraphy and painting are related by a number of criteria, both aesthetic and technical. Some specific examples are provided below.

52 Chao Meng-fu, Yüan dynasty: Sparse Woods and Rocks.

1. Common Points in the Use of the Brush

It has already been mentioned how the different scripts and the different strokes within a single character help determine the manner in which the brush is handled. Another dimension to the use of the brush in calligraphy is composition. Almost all Chinese characters are comprised of various strokes assembled together to form a unit. This is, in essence, an assemblage of lines. In Chinese painting, as we have already noted, line is the single most important element in the description of form. Whether for calligraphy or painting, different brushstrokes result in different effects, depending on the length and thickness of the brush-tip and the stiffness of the hairs. Nonetheless, the fundamental nature of the brush remains constant.

The clearest example of an artist putting into practice the idea of the convertibility of calligraphy and painting is the early Yüan dynasty painter Chao Meng-fu. Chao wrote a poem with the following lines:

> Rocks like "flying-white," trees like seal script;
> In writing bamboo, one must penetrate the eight methods (of calligraphy).
> He who can comprehend this
> Will recognize that calligraphy and painting at root are the same.

Chao Meng-fu was one of the most gifted artists in the history of China and he must have thought deeply before making such an assertion. His painting "Sparse Woods and Rocks" (fig. 52) will help demonstrate the theory. The outline and texturing of the rock in Chao Meng-fu's painting perfectly illustrates the principle of rocks like "flying-white." What is flying-white? When writing calligraphy, the areas within a brushstroke where the brush fails to leave a full measure of ink and streaks of white paper or silk appear is called flying-white. The brush moves quickly to make this flying effect. White is simply the underlying ground that emerges within the stroke. A detail from a famous work of cursive writing by the Northern Sung calligrapher Huang T'ing-chien (1045-1105), "The Biographies of Lien Po and Lin Hsiang-ju" (fig. 53), provides a classic demonstration of this technique. It is precisely the same as seen in the rock of Chao Meng-fu's painting. The flying-white effect results in a highly tactile sensation of the brush's interaction with the paper or silk. This well suits the descriptive goal of the painter, who seeks to convey the rough and weathered texture of the rock. The next comment in Chao Meng-fu's poem is "trees like seal script." An excellent example of seal script writing is seen in a rubbing of the writing of the "Stone Drums" (fig. 54). Each stroke in this calligraphy is round, thick and even—these are qualities associated with antiquity in the aesthetics of Chinese calligraphy, a fact which makes this brush technique particularly well-suited to the description of the branches of aged trees. Chao Meng-fu does not provide any clearer indications of what "penetrating the eight methods for writing bamboo" means. However, clarification appears in a comment written by Chao's younger contemporary K'o Chiu-ssu, a well-known painter who specialized in bamboo:

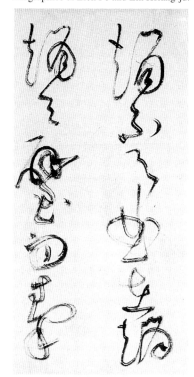

53 Huang T'ing-chien, Sung dynasty: Biographies of Lien Po and Lin Hsiang-ju.

54 Anonymous, Chou dynasty: Rubbing of the Stone Drums.

Above
55 Anonymous, T'ang dynasty:
Figure from the mural paintings in the
tomb of Li Hsien.

Below
56 Anonymous, Ching dynasty:
Rubbing of the stele inscription engraved
at I-shan.

Use the seal script for the stems, the cursive script for the branches and either the clerical script or Yen Chen-ch'ing's style of writing the *p'ieh* slanting stroke for the leaves. For trees and rocks, adopt the idea (in calligraphy) of (strong even turns like) bends in a hairpin and the (random) stains of a leaking roof.

Bamboo leaves flutter and turn like the rising and falling of the inclined strokes of clerical calligraphy. Bamboo branches possess the lively spirit of the quick-moving cursive script. The ultimate indication of calligraphy methods informing painting appears in occasional inscriptions, where the painter uses the character *hsieh*, "to write," in describing his or her painting. It is not uncommon to find the painter speaking of "writing out" the plum blossoms or bamboo.

Variations of brushwork are perhaps clearest in the descriptive lines of figure painting. A figure from the mural paintings found in the T'ang dynasty tomb of Li Hsien demonstrates this point (fig. 55). His shoulders and the outer descriptive lines of his clothing provide a standard example of the so-called iron-wire brushline. A rubbing of the Ch'in dynasty stele inscription engraved at I-shan presents the lesser seal script (fig. 56). The round, perfectly even strokes, with the brush-tip meticulously kept from being exposed, are precisely the same as what are found in the T'ang mural painting. In other words, the iron-wire lines used in the drawing of clothing folds are of the same technique as employed in the writing of the lesser seal script.

Another illustration of the shared techniques of calligraphy and painting is found in a painting of a pomegranate by the Ch'ing dynasty painter Huang Shen (fig. 57), one of the Eight Eccentrics of Yangchou. Branches and leaves were painted at break-neck speed, following the painter's inspiration. The painter's inscription above, written in the cursive script, seemingly extends as a continuation of the slashing lines of the branches. There is no difference in Huang Shen's handling of the brush, from image to inscription.

The brush relies upon ink to leave its traces on paper or silk and the general principle for writing is that a constant tone of ink is easiest on the eyes. Nonetheless, in the writing of calligraphy, there is a ceaseless display of shifting tonal values. The flying-white effect is one example, produced with a relatively dry brush. Other times calligraphers will write a passage without redipping the brush in ink, so that the calligraphy appears increasingly dry until the writer finally stops. In the case of the cursive writing of the Ch'ing dynasty calligrapher Wang To (fig. 58), the brush is first charged with a heavy dose of thick rich ink. The result is a moist, fluid effect that excites the viewer's eye and heart. We have commented on the painter's careful attention to the application of ink. Quite clearly, it is the same for the calligrapher.

Of course, there are differences in the calligrapher's and painter's use of brush and ink: while the characters are of fixed form, the strokes of painting follow the shape of the subject, with the consequence that the shifts and changes of brush and ink will naturally be more varied.

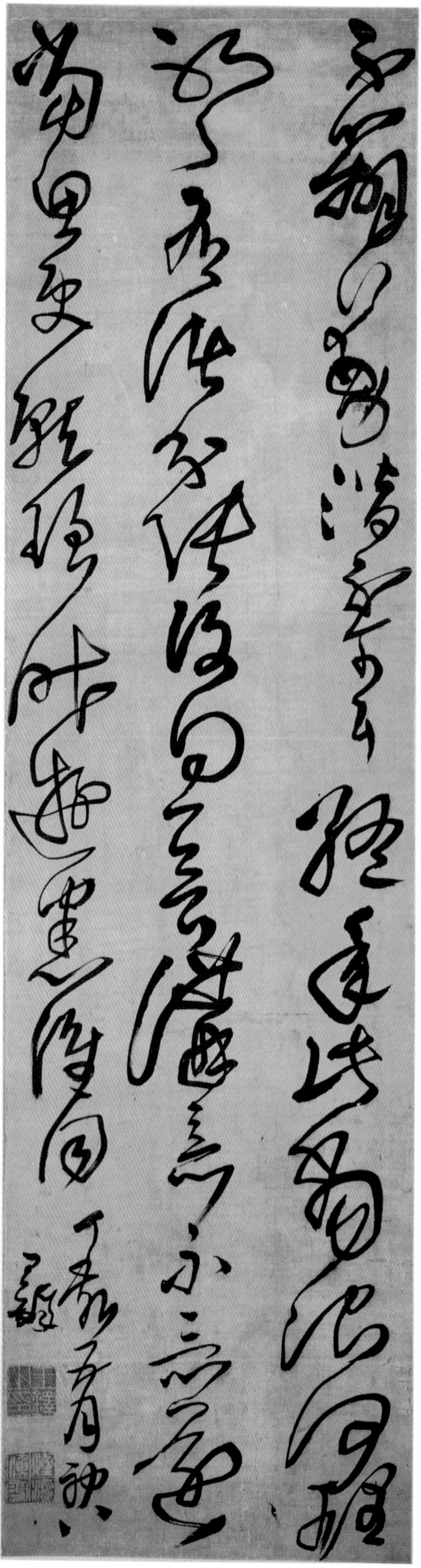

57 Hunag Shen, Ch'ing dynasty:
Pomegranate.

2. Composition

Calligraphy begins with a single stroke or dot, to which others
are joined to form a character. Characters join to form columns;
columns collectively make a composition. Composition begins with
individual characters—the interplay of lines and spaces to form
viable structures. Characters, and the spaces between them, similarly
interact to form a column. Columns have their own manner or air,
depending on the size of its characters, their tilt and density. The total
assemblage of characters in a work of calligraphy is called "the
distribution of columns and arrangement of space." In this regard,

Left
58 Wang To, Ch'ing dynasty:
Calligraphy after Chang chih.

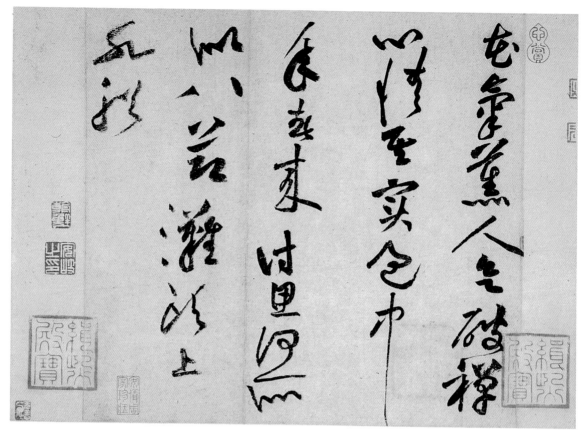

59 Huang T'ing-chien, Sung dynasty: Poem.

compositional practices in calligraphy and painting are largely the same.

A poem on the fragrance of flowers by Huang T'ing-chien will serve as an example (fig. 59). The characters of the first column (from the right) are densely arranged. The second column is comparatively loose, the third dense again and the fourth and fifth loose. The characters tilt one way or the other so that the entire composition gives the impression of a natural process of unwinding and contracting. The T'ang dynasty calligrapher and critic Sun Kuo-t'ing described it most aptly: "With a single dot, the pattern for a character is established; a single character becomes the standard for an entire text." The expansion or contraction of a character begins with the first stroke; a single dot determines how the character will be written. The next character then responds to the previous one and the next one to that one until a column is formed. One column follows in answer to the one before. The principles of composition in painting are similar. The placement of images is carefully considered, their relative distances, angles and directions, as well as the lightness or heaviness of touch in the use of the brush.

When painting relatively complicated compositions, it is not uncommon for the painter first to begin with a draft. When the composition is relatively simple, however, it is often like writing calligraphy, done quickly from beginning to end, one stroke

60 Kuo Hsü, Ming dynasty: Frog and Butterfly.

61 Anonymous, Warring States period: Rubbing of a bell iscription.

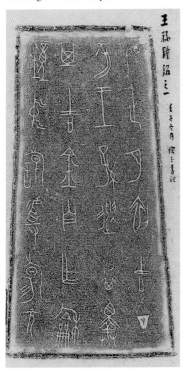

following in reaction to the other, peripheral scenes established in relation to the primary scene. The Ming painter Kuo Hsü's "Frog and Butterfly" (fig. 60) will help illustrate how painting can be similar to calligraphy in this particular respect. Kuo Hsü's initial brush movement appears to have been miscalculated and the artist had to consider how to correct it. The thick green leaf directly above the frog, composed of two brushstrokes, exactly echoes the back of the frog. The reason is that when the artist first thought to paint the frog, his brushstrokes were too thick. If the frog were this large, it would be out of proportion to the size of the painting, which would then be unable to contain the butterfly and other elements of the scene. With consummate skill and quick thinking, Kuo Hsü changed the would-be frog to a leafy plant. Perhaps Kuo Hsü's ability to do this stemmed from the common experience of changing a character midway through writing after realizing that a mistake was being made.

The relationship between painting and calligraphy can also be considered from the perspective of calligraphy being like painting. In painting, the artist focuses on both uniting the picture and enlivening it with transformations. The calligrapher's arrangement of characters and columns is founded on the same principle. Consider, for example, the calligraphy of an inscription taken from a Warring States Period bell (fig. 61). Overall, the writing is slender and elegant, with a resonating air. Each character is constructed with a strong vertical orientation, markedly taller than wide. Moreover, the disposition of strokes is not evenly balanced. Rather, their weight within individual characters tends to be focused either high or low. For example, the character *wang* (second character, second column from the right) is

63 Kuang T'ung, Five dynasties period: Evening Green on Autumn Mountains.

64 Wen Cheng-ming, Ming dynasty: Old Trees by a Cold Stream.

written with two of the horizontal strokes concentrated at the top, while *chi* (directly facing to the left) has a low center of gravity with the two horizontal strokes pressing down upon the bottom of the character. More than simply elements of design, arrangements such as these can be considered painting-like compositions.

3. "Idea-realm" and "Body-spirit"

The third aspect shared between painting and calligraphy is of an aesthetic nature. The overall impression that a painting presents is what was called its "breath-resonance" (*ch'i-yun*) in the past and is now referred to as its "idea-realm" (*i-ching*). What of calligraphy? By habit, the term used is *feng-shen*, the physicality and spirit of the writing, or what might be translated as "body-spirit." Although difficult to describe, the term refers to the sense of strength that emanates from an individual work of calligraphy. Whether it is the shapes and colors of a painting or the interacting strokes of calligraphy, collectively these elements come together and convey an essence or spirit: "idea-realm" and "body-spirit." It is often said that one's calligraphy is just like the person. Calligraphy expresses a sense of that individual precisely because its body-spirit is like the writer. In some cases it may be heroic and strong, other times refined and untrammeled, forthright and virile, or wild and unrestrained. Its attraction is not necessarily pleasing to the eye; charm may stem from some idiosyncrasy or imbalance. In this regard, the variations of individual expression in calligraphy closely resemble the various idea-realms of painting. For an example, we choose a detail from the T'ang calligrapher Yen Chen-ch'ing's "Stele of the Yen Family Ancestral Temple" (fig. 62). The calligraphy emanates an air of strength and honesty. The viewer senses the immovable stability of a mountain, like the majestic Mount T'ai of Shantung Province. The overall impression calls to mind the great landscape paintings of the Northern Sung period—something like "Evening Green on Autumn Mountains" (fig. 63), which is attributed to the tenth century painter Kuan T'ung. This is the hard, virile landscape of north China and it provides a fitting complement to the formidable presence of Yen Chen-ch'ing's calligraphy. For another example, we return to Huang T'ing-chien's calligraphy (fig. 59). Huang's writing is characterized by long brushstrokes—what one critic described as "long spears and great halberds." To the viewer, the impression is of a gangly, long-limbed fellow happily stretching his arms and legs in some sort of improvised jig. Something similar is sensed from "Old Trees by a Cold Stream" by the Ming painter Wen Cheng-ming (fig. 64). Pine and cypress intertwine, one leaning upon the other. The trunk of the cypress is old and weathered, its branches revolving in all directions. The pine, in contrast, shoots directly upward. Like Huang T'ing-chien's calligraphy, such uninhibited expression of movement and emotion gives the impression of joyful dance. Looking at such a painting, one feels that nothing restrains us. The world is limitless, awaiting our high-stepping wanderings.

62 Yen Chen-ch'ing, T'ang dynasty: Rubbing of the stele of the Yen Family Ancestral Temple.

Chapter Seven
The Merging of Poetry and Painting
"A painting within the poem, a poem within the painting"

There are paintings that single-mindedly pursue the beauties of form and color with little, if any, consideration of the meanings that might be suggested by its subject. Some call this pure painting, but it is not what one finds in Chinese painting. The Chinese painter's rock or bamboo or orchid is, on the one hand, an expression of formal beauty. But these things are also objects of metaphorical significance. Commonly, an accompanying inscription will praise the numinous spirit of the rock, or extol the lofty purity of the bamboo or orchid. In this manner, Chinese painting becomes more than a medium of pure description and interacts with literature, especially poetry. The Cubists focused on the organization of formal geometric shapes. Purely abstract painters, even more so than Cubists, are concerned with lines and colors that have no representational function. This can be called the limits of pure painting. In contrast, Chinese painters from the ancient past to recent times felt compelled to inscribe poetry on their paintings. Two modes of expression result: image and word. As the common phrase goes, "Within the poem is a painting, and within the painting is a poem."

Poetry is an art of words and sounds; painting is an art of forms and colors. Their modes of expression are entirely different. How do the two unite in Chinese painting? This is the question that we must pursue.

Looking back over the history of Chinese painting, the figure who is inevitably associated with the concept of *ut pictura poesis* is Wang Wei of the T'ang dynasty. Wang Wei himself joked that he was one "who in this life mistakenly became a man of letters; in a former life I must have been a painting master." Unfortunately, Wang Wei's paintings have not survived, but his poems are commonly quoted and among them one finds lines with images that seemingly evoke beautiful painted scenes:

The moon shines among the pines;
A clear stream flows over the rocks.

Reversing shadows enter the deep forest grove;
Returning glows ascend the green moss.

Of course, Wang Wei was not the only one to specialize in poetry descriptive of scenery, but in the history of China there were few like him who were able to combine exceptional talents as both a poet and a painter.

The merging of poetry and painting goes back a long ways in China. If one speaks of "poems with paintings within," then there are numerous examples whose images seem to linger in the mind of the reader, beginning with the earliest anthology of poetry in China, the

Shih-ching. A more direct connection between the two arts is found in poems written specifically for paintings by the High T'ang poets Li Po (701-762) and Tu Fu (712-70). These, however, are usually poems the poet was inspired to write after appreciating a painting. It was not yet common practice to inscribe poems directly on paintings. Paintings remained paintings; poems remained poems. While connections could be made between the two, they were far from being integrated.

The person who most clearly promoted the concept of paintings in poems and poems in paintings was Su Shih (1036-1101) of the Northern Sung. A comment that Su Shih wrote to the effect that Wang Wei's poems and paintings possessed these interlocking qualities was largely responsible for the T'ang figure's transformation into one who embodied the merging of the two arts. The same idea underlies two lines of a poem Su Shih wrote for a painting of horses by the T'ang painter Han Kan: "Shao-ling's (Tu Fu's) brush and ink create a formless painting; Han Kan's reds and blues are a wordless poem." Su Shih's slightly younger contemporary Huang T'ing-chien had this to say about the painting of a mutual friend, Li Kung-lin: "Lord Li has verses that refuse to be uttered, so he uses light ink to sketch out a soundless poem." During the Sung and Yüan dynasties, many of the educated elite known as the literati adopted painting as an avocation and their efforts, as well as their critiques of painting, largely possessed ideas borrowed from literature. Over time, so fully does the relationship between poetry and painting become integrated that "soundless poem" develops into a common sobriquet for painting. One book on painting, the early Ch'ing author Chiang Shao-shu's study of Ming painters, even uses this phrase for its title: *A History of Soundless Poems*.

Poetry proves to be an important source of inspiration for the Chinese painter. Already in the Northern Sung, the great landscape artist Kuo Hsi commented on the benefits a painter could gain from reading broadly: "Recite the pure lines and elegant verses of the men of antiquity. Among them are those that inspire fine thoughts and can be painted." Kuo Hsi goes on to record a number of poetic lines he considers suitable for painting—an indication of how highly valued poetry was as a source for painting themes. Shortly after Kuo Hsi, the idea of "poems within paintings" was taken a step further with the promotion of the use of poetry in the examinations of academy painters at the Northern Sung court. Poetic lines were chosen as subjects for painting, with the painters left to their own devices to express the poetic idea in their compositions. Here is an example of one set of lines that was used:

Tender green on branch-tips, a touch of red,
It takes little for spring colors to vex the heart.

Most of the painters who illustrated these lines painted rich flowering trees with the intention of conveying the brilliance of spring. The painter who earned top honors, however, was much more subtle. He offered a scene of willow trees and a high tower. Leaning on the balustrade, looking into the distance with thoughts of her lover, was depicted a beautiful young woman whose mouth was painted with a touch of red. Using the red of the maiden's lips to suggest the vexing

65 Hsü Ti, Sung dynasty: Insects and Wild Grasses.

colors of spring allowed this artist's painting, in the minds of the judges, to best approximate the essence of the poem.

Enveloped by bamboo at the side of the bridge, a wine-seller's house.

In this case, the examinees all worked hard to describe a rustic wine shop. The one exception was Li T'ang, a painter destined to be one of the greatest of the period. All he painted was the bamboo beyond the bridge and a solitary banner wafting in the wind above with the single character for wine written upon it. His interpretation conveyed the idea of the wine shop enveloped by bamboo.

Treading the flowers returning home, horse hooves are fragrant.

The perfume of flowers is something sensed by the nose, not the eyes, and hence difficult to portray in painting. The best painting in this case depicted a group of butterflies chasing after a horse's trotting hooves, which carry with them the fleeing fragrance.

Choosing an old poem as the subject for one's composition is called painting "poetic ideas," *shih-i*. Examples of this practice abound in Chinese painting. Sometimes a line from a poem is inscribed on the painting after it is finished in order to intensify the meanings of the painting. How a poem can add to a painting's appreciation is demonstrated by Ma Lin's "Night Outing with Candles" (fig. 37). This fan painting has been proved to be an illustration of the following lines of a poem by Su Shih: "My fear is that in the depths of night, the flowers will fall asleep and depart, so I light the tall candles to illuminate their red beauty." Doesn't the viewer gain an added element of pleasure once the painting's poetic ideas are understood? Among all of the arts, literature is the most broadly appreciated, for it uses words and writing as its medium—that which is studied by everyone from an early age. Writing is something easily comprehended. There is no need for specialized training. Hence, when poems and paintings are joined together, the viewer's appreciation and understanding are enhanced by the poetic text. After the Yüan dynasty, literati painting flourished and the merging of poem and painting became accepted as perfectly natural.

Our examination into the relationship, however, should proceed a step further. Inscribing a poem on a painting provides a kind of guide to the viewer, but painting and poem remain united only on the surface. If the painter always relied upon poetry for sources of illustration, the painting would be reduced to a supporting role for literature. A painter uses forms and colors to express poetic feelings and if we are to seek the manner in which the painter uses his "color-brush" to write a soundful poem, then we must determine the ways in which his forms, colors and "idea-realm" allow poem and painting to merge in a more intrinsic, meaningful manner.

What the Chinese painter describes with mountain, water, rock and tree, using his or her skills of composition, description and color, is oftentimes a dream-like realm beyond the grasp of common experience. Painter and poet alike fill their hearts with thoughts of reclusion and escape the problems of the mundane world by retreating to their studio, where paper or silk can be spread and a more perfect world can be explored. Amid serried peaks, deep in the white clouds, a remote and peaceful residence...deep gorges, towering pines, waterfalls and strange rocks. Here one can sing in harmony with nature and dispel one's frustrations, forever separated from the dusty world. How different is this world created by the painter from the world of the poet?

The viewer, of course, may not be able to see what the painter sees, experience what the painter experiences, but through this painting, we catch a glimpse of the artist's world, just as we appreciate spectacular scenery seen from our car windows. Scenes flash by, ungraspable but for an instant, yet our hearts are stirred by the beauty. The poet uses words and sounds to sing his or her emotions. The painter uses "reds and blues" to sketch his or her impressions. Yet both, in that moment of inspiration, are filled with the joy described by the lines, "Heaven and earth enter my heart, objects and images are my own design." There is an affirmation of the self as the artist creates and it matters not whether it is a poet or a painter—the realm that exists in their hearts is of one kind only. Beginning with that initial moment of inspiration, poetry and painting are both art and art arises from the emotions formed by what is seen, heard and considered. We might say that the former is the expression of feelings while the latter is the expression of images. When the images of a scene are encountered, the poet's feelings are born. Relying on feelings, the painter's images are created. Yet, this is not to say that all poems and paintings possess this realm where feelings and scene fuse as one. Let us look more closely at this relationship between emotion and scene and provide some specific examples.

1. The Handling of Poetic Space

In Sung painting, or more specifically, in Southern Sung painting, there is a vital energy that permeates the air of serene remoteness. It is just as Li Ch'ing-chao (1084-?) wrote in one of her poems: "Mountain light and water hues, intimate with me." All is filled with a sense of emotion. This is the true merging of object with person.

Earlier we cited the lines of Meng Chiao (751-814), "Heaven and earth enter my breast; objects and images are my own design," to emphasize the painter's role as creator. To this, we add another phrase that reflects upon the artist's ability to control all time and space in the palm of his or her hand: "Past and present absorbed in a flash; (all between) the four seas stroked in an instant." The artist's heart "roams the river between heaven and earth," and objects can emerge magically "between the form and nothingness of mountains' hues." In the first chapter, the question "Where does one search for the pavilions of immortal mountains?" was shown to reflect upon the painter's basic task of abstracting and recomposing to make a painting. It can also be used to describe the methods of the poet. The Chinese painter utilizes the subtle possibilities of the unpainted areas of the painting to establish the illusion of space, and he uses an unfixed perspective to cut and assemble the most beautiful scenes. This is the synthesis of "the many places where the body has lingered, the (profound) sights to which the eye has been drawn," as Tsung Ping described in "Preface on Landscape Painting." Here is a verse by a poet active in the early years of the Southern Sung. Reading it and then looking back at some of the paintings already discussed, is not what the poet describes similar to what is seen in the paintings?

> Filling one's eyes, the waters of the long river;
> Richly verdant, the mountains of an unknown prefecture.
> The hastening of ten thousand miles,
> All in the frame of a single window.　　—Ch'en Yü-i (1090-1138)

The poem's broad field of vision, the landscape contained in "the frame of a window," includes ten thousand miles of mountains and rivers. This is not something that can be captured in the single release of a camera's shutter. Rather, it is more like the overall impression received from the panorama of a film on landscape. The handling of space in painting and poem is essentially the same.

2. Poetic Emotions in Painting

In the line of verse, "Red apricot blossoms at the branch's tip—the clamor of spring," the poetic idea all hinges upon the single character *nao*, "clamor." Similarly, in the line, "Clouds come breaking the moon, flowers sport with their shadows," the character *nung*, "sport" or "play," carries the idea-realm of the poem. The emotions of spring on a moonlit night are all entrusted to these two characters. In poetry, attention focuses on the merging of emotion (*ch'ing*) and scene (*ching*). Painting only has form and color with which to express an emotional state. How form and color can be used to emphasize such things becomes the issue. Bird-and-flower paintings tend to offer the best illustration of this because the scene is generally limited in scope. Unlike the breadth of landscape's illusion, the world of the single flower is like a photographic close-up. In the details, one perceives how a painting is able to convey the kinds of effects that the characters for "clamor" and "sport" provide in the poetic lines cited above.

For an example, we choose the Southern Sung painter Hsü Ti's "Insects and Wild Grasses" (fig. 65). The composition is exceedingly simple: a butterfly and dragonfly hover above a single stem of Chinese cabbage and a grasshopper on the ground. The four elements are placed evenly on the surface of the silk fan, resulting in a rather stiff arrangement. However, such is the painter's ability to convey the spirit of each of the motifs that the viewer takes little notice of the composition's shortcomings. The outlines of the vegetable's stems and leaves were carefully delineated in ink while varied tones of green pigment were used for an interior wash. Lastly, white powdered pigment was applied from the stems to the tips of the leaf veins. The spatial disposition of the leaves, with their turns and folds, is well described, imparting a marvelous sense of life. One of the lower leaves is gone, leaving only half a stem. Another one bends to the ground, its edge browning with decay. They contrast with the other leaves, which in turn seem all the more alive. Dragonfly, butterfly and grasshopper are equally well-described, frozen, it seems, in the middle of their movements. Colors and forms well elicit the painting's emotional quality with a sense of life's vitality. In effect, if not method, we can say that they function the same as those key characters "clamor" and "sport" do in the poet's verse.

In Chinese painting, the idea, rather than the object, is important and in order to emphasize feelings, to bring its spirit to life, the artist must use his or her imagination in addition to descriptive skills. For example, a poet writes of his white hair growing three thousand yards long, but of course, this is something unseen in the real world. In a similar vein, one often sees in Chinese paintings images of longevity figures with impossibly large heads. This is the artist's solution for expressing the figure's great age. If correct proportions were followed, the painter may not be able to convey the idea of white hair that was three thousand yards long.

3. The Idea beyond the Image, the Flavor beyond the Words

In expressing ideas in painting, the Chinese artist often speaks of "capturing it beyond the image." To put this another way, when appreciating an excellent painting, we seem to be led to thoughts and emotions that exist beyond the painted forms. In poetry, more often, it is the "flavor beyond the words." The idea beyond the image, the flavor beyond the words. How could these two things not be related? The focus in Chinese landscape painting is on creating a scene and the painter's scene is often related to the poet's scene. Consider, for example, the Ming master Shen Chou's "Walking with a Staff" (fig. 66). The style of the painting follows that of the Yüan artist Ni Tsan (see Figure 11), with each stroke and dot precisely executed in a full display of Shen Chou's skill. By a lakeside bank walks a scholar with a staff. The atmosphere of the painting is precisely as Shen Chou describes in his poetic inscription: "Mountains quiet, like great antiquity." In fact, the mountains are so quiet one can almost hear the sounds of leaves growing. Two lines from a Wang Wei poem are reminiscent of this pure, dreamlike world: "Amid the rain, fruit falls from the mountain tree; under the lantern, grass insects sing." In both painting and poem, we sense the emotions that exist beyond the objects. Quite a number of Chinese paintings share this characteristic. That is to say, the spirit of poetry and painting can be remarkably close. Sketching a scene is the same as sketching feelings. Even if the elements sketched are material objects, what is most important is the painting's idea-realm. Painting is not simply a matter of relaying visual impressions that are received by the eye; rather, it is the merging of impressions with emotions. Because of this, one could say that the expression "a poem within the painting" is essentially a comment on the identicalness of the realms of these two arts.

Similarities between painting and poetry are not limited to these observations, but if forced to summarize, one would conclude that the poet's methods of composition are like those of the painter. The poet uses the painter's sharp and inspired eye to create a poem that presents its own world. As for the painter, is his wielding of the brush not like the writing of beautiful words and phrases? With it, he or she creates forms and colors capable of expressing the crystal clarity of a poet's feelings. We say that poetry is an expression of the heart. Literati painters say something similar: my painting gives vent to the untrammeled spirit contained in my breast.

66 Shen Chou, Ming dynasty: Walking with a Staff.

Chapter Eight

The Presentation of Chinese Painting
Inscriptions, seals and mounting

Differences between Chinese and Western painting are many indeed, but if only two were to be singled out as being particularly conspicuous, they would have to be the propensity of Chinese painters to write lengthy inscriptions on their paintings and the habit of impressing seals upon them. Painting is form and color. Writing may at root also be an art of modeled forms, but more prominently, it is a medium that expresses thoughts and ideas with fixed meanings. Seals are symbols of trust impressed upon documents as a form of proof. How these three different forms of art unite in Chinese painting is the main focus of this chapter.

◀ Fan K'uan's signature

1. Signatures and Inscriptions

Early Chinese painting was no different from Western painting in that the painted image itself was the only concern. Painting was painting, not something to be mixed with other elements. Never mind inscribed poems. Even the artist's signature was customarily hidden from sight. The great majority of extant paintings from the Sung period are unsigned and those few that are may be inscribed in such subtle places as the fissure of a rock or the trunk of a tree. It is not that the artist was particularly modest, hiding his identity from obvious view. Rather, there was the fear that a conspicuous signature would interfere with the painting's unity, perhaps disrupt the believability of the scene.

A few examples will illustrate, beginning with Fan K'uan's "Travelers among Mountains and Streams." The two characters of Fan K'uan's name are written among the leaves in the lower right-hand corner of the painting (figs. 67, 68.1). These small characters are absolutely minuscule when considered in relation to the total size of the painting, which is over six feet tall, and if not pointed out, it is highly unlikely that the viewer would ever see Fan K'uan's signature. Kuo Hsi signed, dated and titled his painting "Early Spring" of 1072 at the center of the left border and added a seal reading "Brush of Kuo Hsi" (fig. 13, 68.2). At the very end of the Northern Sung, Li T'ang signed "Whispering Pines in the Gorges" with the short inscription "Painted by Li T'ang of Ho-yang in spring of the *chia-chen* year of the Hsüan-ho reign of our Emperor (1124)." His signature appears on a distant needle-like peak just to the left of the central mountain (fig. 33, 68.3). The Southern Sung painter Chia Shih-ku inscribed the three characters of his name on the lower slope of his landscape fan (fig. 68.4).

The close relationship between painting and calligraphy has already been discussed in a previous chapter. There are, however,

67 Fan K'uan, Sung dynasty: Travelers among Mountains and Streams (detail).

additional factors to consider with regard to the emphasis Chinese place on the convertibility of these two arts. Chinese painting after the Sung commonly utilizes the bare, untouched ground of the silk or paper to suggest an expanse of background sky or water. In the Southern Sung and Yüan, this "remaining white" (*liu-pai*), as it is called, absorbs an increasingly large proportion of the painting. This becomes the stage for the artist's inscription, which is added to enhance the painting. It could be a poem, or it could be a prose inscription somehow related to the making of the painting. Of course, there is a more important dimension to the text beyond the interest of its content and that is the calligraphy, the style of which must be carefully considered to harmonize with the painting. The calligraphy may be written with restrained, sensuous grace, or it may be written with a wildly splashing, dancing brush. In all cases, however, it is essential that the calligraphy be well-written and that it agrees with the painting. If one's calligraphic skills are lacking, it is better that the painting be left alone. It is for this reason that teachers often tell would-be students of painting to practice calligraphy first. When a fine painting is paired with an "unsympathetic" inscription, it is like a beautiful, carefully adorned woman who suddenly develops an unsightly blemish on her face.

2. Seals

T'ang and Sung painters commonly hid their signatures in obscure places and they rarely used seals. The many seals now seen on such early paintings almost always belong to later collectors, both private and imperial. In almost all cases, the artists would not have seen these collectors' seals, nor would they have necessarily condoned them.

68.1
Fan K'uan's signature

68.2
Kuo Hsi's signature

68.3
Li T'ang's signature

68.4
Chia Shih-ku's signature

69.1
Shih-t'ao's seal

69.2
Shih-t'ao's seal

69.3
Pa-ta shan-jen's seal

69.4
Ch'i Pai-shih's seal

When we view paintings on exhibit at the National Palace Museum, one notes immediately the countless seals of various sizes that often cover a painting, sometimes to the detriment of the painting's expression of space. They are not unlike the unlicensed buildings that are sometimes constructed without care or thought in an otherwise beautiful city.

Seals have been used in China since very early in its history. Those of the Ch'in and Han dynasties are now considered exemplary models by those who carve seals today. On contemporary paintings and calligraphy, seal impressions are an element that is never missing. The carving of seals is now recognized as an independent art and when well-placed on a painting's surface, there is no doubt that seals can enhance the overall effect of a painting. In this respect, seals are just like calligraphic inscriptions. They stimulate the eye and add another dimension to one's appreciation. Painting, writing and seals all mutually gain from one another. The content of seals can also enhance a painting. For example, the early Ch'ing dynasty individualist painter Shih-t'ao used a seal that reads, "Scouring the earth in search of strange peaks for my painting drafts" (fig. 69.1). This well illustrates what was discussed earlier, that the painter's unusual scenery has its roots in actual landscape and what appears in his paintings is the assembled fruits of extensive sojourns and experience. Another seal by Shih-t'ao reads, "Excelling at idiocy" (fig. 69.2), which indicates an element of humor in his paintings that the viewer should be ready to enjoy. Pa-ta shan-jen used a seal that reads, "Attaining immortality" (fig. 69.3). Such seals bring an element of immediacy to the viewer's appreciation; they enjoin us to imagine the artist finishing his painting, setting aside the brush and impressing the seal, thus bringing this undertaking to a close. The twentieth century master Ch'i Pai-shih excelled at carving seals. To his large, freely sketched paintings of flowers, he would add a seal of equally bold appearance. For autumn scenes, he had a seal that reads "Thinking of the red leaves of Nung Mountain," and for paintings of spring flowers, "The mountain flowers of home bloom this time of year" (fig. 69.4). The sentimental thoughts of home evoked by these seals impart a romantic air to Ch'i Pai-shih's paintings. In this respect, the legends of seals can play an analogous role to poetic inscriptions.

Ancient seals were all carved from relatively hard materials, such as jade, ivory, bronze and bone, and for a long time, most painters and calligraphers relied on skilled craftsmen to carve seals that they had first designed. At the end of the Yüan dynasty, Wang Mien, who specialized in the painting of plum blossoms, began to use a soft stone called *hua-ju-shih* for his seals. An everyday steel knife could be used and from this time forward, many artists began to rely on their own talents to carve seals. The result was a blossoming of styles and manners, from the most meticulous to the most abandoned. With this creative freedom came a broader application for seals. In the middle of the Ming dynasty, the calligrapher and painter Wen P'eng began using stones from Ch'ing-t'ien in Chekiang Province. This stone continues to be used today.

Why do painters like to use seals? And why do they lavish so much attention on them? Ink painting has formed the dominant stream within

Chinese painting since the T'ang and Sung dynasties. Close your eyes and imagine for a moment the black-and-white world of monochrome painting. Pure and unsoiled, almost inevitably the painting will possess a light, calm air. Now add to this the brilliant, passionate vermilion of a seal impression, whose position on the painting surface is first carefully plotted. The effect is as attractive as a pair of crimson lips adorning the unblemished porcelain face of a young maiden. Once this effect that a seal can make is recognized, one always feels unsatisfied to look at a painting with only the artist's signature but no seal.

The combining of calligraphy and seals with a painting is like a great chef assembling dishes at an elegant meal. To begin with, the painting must be excellent. The calligraphy cannot be carelessly written and the seals must not be carelessly impressed. With regard to assembling these three, we borrow the well-known phrase of a Ch'ing dynasty critic: "Inscription, position and painting-realm." These are the foundation. The painter leads the viewer into a different, magical realm from the one we know. It is a world of myriad possible variations, each one determined by the artist's handling of composition and structure. The same hill and valley, grass and tree can produce different scenes depending on how they are arranged. Inscriptions are also important elements to be considered in one's composition, and although seals and their application are not mentioned in the phrase just cited as the foundation for painting, they too must be considered as a part of the overall composition. To illustrate this, we turn to an album leaf painting of vegetables by the early Ch'ing dynasty artist Ch'uan-ch'i, otherwise known as Pa-ta shan-jen (fig. 70). Cabbage and leaves are centered high in the composition. One stem slants toward the lower left. Accompanying this rather simple arrangement is a single artist's seal in the lower right corner. The legend, in intaglio, reads, "A person of the Pure Land." On the one hand, the seal indicates that the artist is a Buddhist adept, but it also plays an important role in the painting's composition. Without it, the lower right corner of the painting would

70 Ch'uan-ch'i, Ch'ing dynasty: Cabbage.

become too empty and there would be nothing to balance the dipping stem of the cabbage. A collector's seal carved with fine characters is also seen in the lower left corner: "Authenticated by Sung Chih." This seal does not count as the bothersome type and it has little effect on the balance of solids and voids in the painting.

Figure 71 presents "The High, High Pavilion" by the Yüan dynasty painter Fang Ts'ung-i. The artist inscribed the title in four characters written in clerical script at the upper right. Along the left border, he added an inscription in two columns written in the draft-cursive style. This is what originally accompanied the painting. Calligraphy and painted imagery do not interfere with one another. Moreover, the artist left a relatively broad expanse of paper at the top for sky, which allows the mountains to soar upward. The tone of the calligraphy well matches the painting. Unfortunately, once this painting entered the hands of the Ch'ing dynasty emperor Ch'ien-lung, its appearance changed. A huge square seal reading "Treasure of Ch'ien-lung's imperial viewing" was impressed at the top of the very center of the painting, blocking the vital flow of vertical space. It is as hideous as a large poultice of medicine stuck to someone's forehead. Most of the smaller seals stamped along the two sides of the painting also belong to the Ch'ing dynasty court. These help establish the fact that the painting entered the imperial collection sometime prior to the eighteenth century, but that is about the extent of their usefulness.

To illustrate how seals need not deface a painting, I recount a recent anecdote. In 1933, paintings and calligraphy of the National Palace Museum were moved from Beijing to Shanghai. A year later, the Education Department delegated agents to help oversee the inspection and inventory. On the outer silk or paper mounting, a single seal was stamped: "Seal of inspection by the Education Department." There is a simple reason why this seal was placed on the mountings rather than the paintings, as was the habit of previous collectors. These earlier seals were like illegal structures and there was no point in continuing a bad practice. It is said that the person in charge from the Education Department still wished to put the seals directly on the paintings. His argument was that a seal on the outer mounting was no guarantee against a possible replacement with a forgery. All one had to do was remove the mounting, seal and all, and attach it to the fake—the so-called "golden cicada molting its shell." The National Palace Museum staff, however, thought that the painting surfaces should not be touched. They proposed stamping the backs of the paintings. In the end, a compromise was reached and the Education Department's seal was impressed at the lower left corners of the fronts of the scrolls.

Besides the artist's own seals on a painting, one also sees those of the colophon writers. Most common are collectors' seals, from which we can often tell who owned the painting. There is a common saying: "Outsiders see a commotion, but insiders recognize the gateway." The appreciation of Chinese painting and calligraphy is just like this. Numerous seals on a painting or work of calligraphy naturally give an impression of visual complexity and noise to the painting's or writing's atmosphere. Yet, these seals often prove valuable by telling us who previously owned the painting. Over a long period of time an ancient painting or calligraphy will naturally change ownership many

71 Fang Ts'ung-i, Yüan dynasty: The High, High Pavilion.

times. If the various collectors impress their seals, then later viewers can piece together the history of the scroll's transmission. If there are other sources to be consulted, such as inscriptions and textual records, then our knowledge is further enhanced. All these materials can be utilized to provide the painting with its own record of birth and maturity. An old painting with its pedigree established is naturally worth many times its weight in gold.

3. Mounting

After the painting is completed, an inscription is added and seals are impressed, it still remains for the painting to be mounted before it can be appreciated hanging on the wall or unrolled on a table. Mounting is also the key to preserving paintings and calligraphy. One could say that the quality of a mounting, its materials, design and format, all have a direct bearing on a painting's expressive character. Mounting is the adornment of painting and calligraphy and in this respect can be likened to the clothes that we wear. In China, not only does mounting demand the skilled techniques of specialists, it should also be considered an art by itself. From the fifth century of the Six Dynasties Period, many have devoted their attention to this craft. To the present day, it is still valued as an essential part of painting and calligraphy.

The mounting of painting and calligraphy can be said to combine both the demands of appreciation and preservation. Unrolled or opened, a scroll or album leaf can be hung on the wall or spread open on a table; rolled or folded and it is easily stored and transported. This is one of the special characteristics of Chinese painting and calligraphy. Various changes have taken place in the techniques and formats of mounting over the centuries, but in general, there are only three main types: hanging scrolls, handscrolls and album leaves. More recently, one also sees individual pieces mounted and set to frames. The screen is a format which combines hanging scrolls together and the *heng-p'i*, or hanging handscroll, allows relatively short handscrolls to be seen in their entirety at once. Diagrams of various mounting formats and their individual elements are appended here (fig. 72), so little more need be said except to point out that there is much room for variation within any particular format depending on one's preferences. The formats, in other words, are not rigidly fixed.

72 Mounting formats

1. Single-color mounting hanging scroll

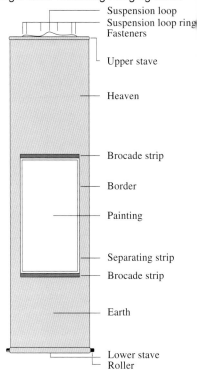

- Suspension loop
- Suspension loop ring
- Fasteners
- Upper stave
- Heaven
- Brocade strip
- Border
- Painting
- Separating strip
- Brocade strip
- Earth
- Lower stave
- Roller

2. Two-color mounting hanging scroll

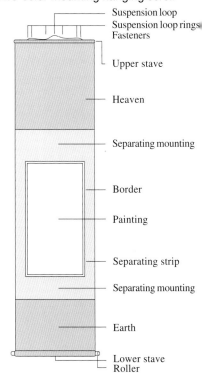

- Suspension loop
- Suspension loop rings
- Fasteners
- Upper stave
- Heaven
- Separating mounting
- Border
- Painting
- Separating strip
- Separating mounting
- Earth
- Lower stave
- Roller

3. Three-color mounting hanging scroll

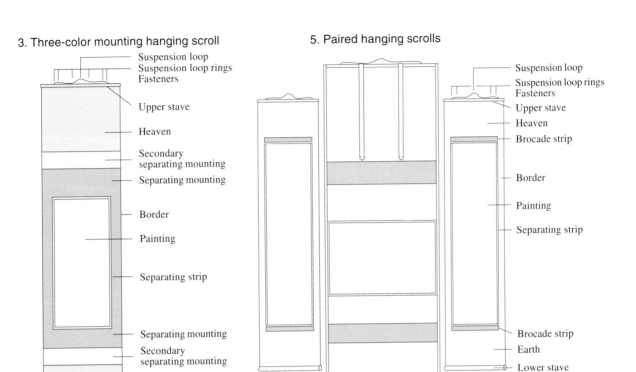

- Suspension loop
- Suspension loop rings
- Fasteners
- Upper stave
- Heaven
- Secondary separating mounting
- Separating mounting
- Border
- Painting
- Separating strip
- Separating mounting
- Secondary separating mounting
- Earth
- Lower stave
- Roller

5. Paired hanging scrolls

- Suspension loop
- Suspension loop rings
- Fasteners
- Upper stave
- Heaven
- Brocade strip
- Border
- Painting
- Separating strip
- Brocade strip
- Earth
- Lower stave

4. Sung-style mounting hanging scroll

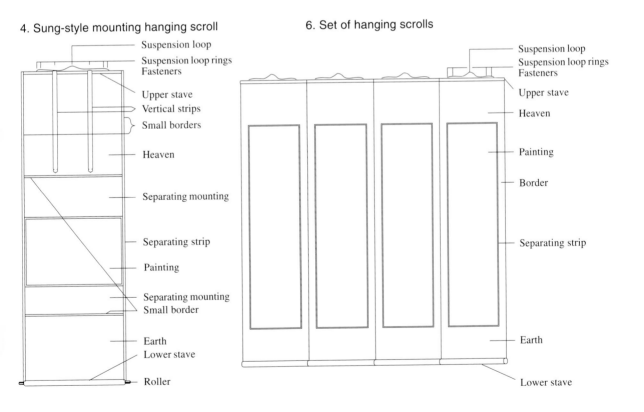

- Suspension loop
- Suspension loop rings
- Fasteners
- Upper stave
- Vertical strips
- Small borders
- Heaven
- Separating mounting
- Separating strip
- Painting
- Separating mounting
- Small border
- Earth
- Lower stave
- Roller

6. Set of hanging scrolls

- Suspension loop
- Suspension loop rings
- Fasteners
- Upper stave
- Heaven
- Painting
- Border
- Separating strip
- Earth
- Lower stave

7. Back side of a hanging scroll

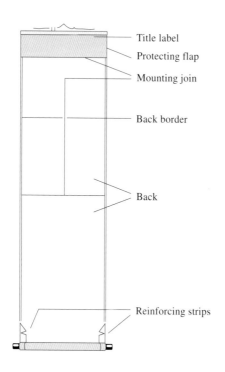

- Title label
- Protecting flap
- Mounting join
- Back border
- Back
- Reinforcing strips

8. Upper stave of a hanging scroll

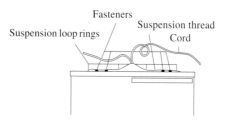

- Suspension loop rings
- Fasteners
- Suspension thread
- Cord

9. Screen

10. Handscroll

Backside of a handscroll

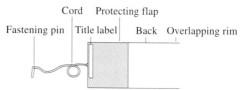

- Fastening pin
- Cord
- Title label
- Protecting flap
- Back
- Overlapping rim

1 Large border handscroll

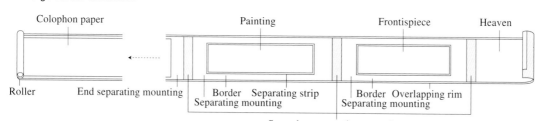

- Colophon paper
- Painting
- Frontispiece
- Heaven
- Roller
- End separating mounting
- Border
- Separating strip
- Separating mounting
- Border
- Overlapping rim
- Separating mounting
- Secondary separating mountings

2 Small border handscroll

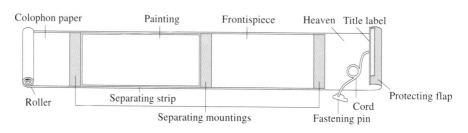

- Colophon paper
- Painting
- Frontispiece
- Heaven
- Title label
- Roller
- Separating strip
- Separating mountings
- Cord
- Fastening pin
- Protecting flap

11. Horizontal hanging scroll

1 Two-color mounting horizontal hanging scroll with ivory rollers

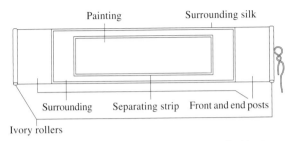

Painting   Surrounding silk

Surrounding   Separating strip   Front and end posts

Ivory rollers

2 Single-color mounting horizontal hanging scroll with staves

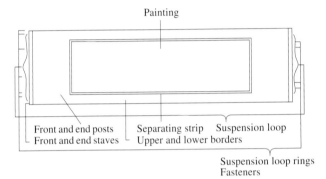

Painting

Front and end posts   Separating strip   Suspension loop
Front and end staves   Upper and lower borders

Suspension loop rings
Fasteners

12. Small painting mountings

Two-color mounting for horizontal paintings

One-color mounting for vertical paintings

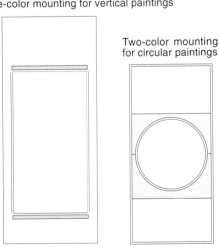

Two-color mounting
for circular paintings

13. Accordion album

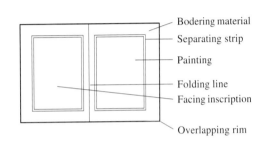

Bodering material

Separating strip

Painting

Folding line
Facing inscription

Overlapping rim

14. Transverse album

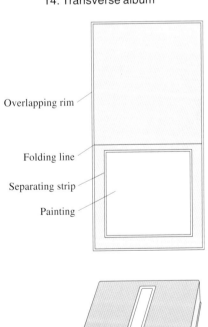

Overlapping rim

Folding line

Separating strip

Painting

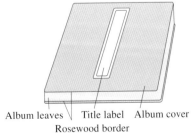

Album leaves   Title label   Album cover
Rosewood border

鄰惠無疆雖莫論集岩巖兀立鼎常存萬桔華插根能結富貴榮華到子孫

己未秋十月一日吳昌碩老缶筆七十六

海上禪甓軒

Chapter Nine
Playing with Brush and Ink
Unusual Techniques in Chinese Painting

As the saying goes, to be good at something, you must first sharpen your tools. For Chinese painting and calligraphy, the weapon of choice is the brush, whose round, drill-shaped head distinguishes it from the kind of brush used for oil painting. Other materials are paper, silk, ink and water soluble pigments. For the artist, what is most important is to utilize these tools and materials in such a manner that they express his or her ideas. As for one's particular techniques, the painter plays the role of Creator. Tools and materials can be used in various ways to elicit unusual effects. What counts is that the viewer's own interest and understanding be stimulated. When this occurs, an excellent work of art results. Painting is an act of creative freedom and while the vast majority of painters in China use the standard brush to pursue their art, there are exceptions. This chapter will serve to introduce some of these unorthodox techniques.

74 P'u Hsin-yü, 20th century: Buffaloes Fording a Stream.

1. Finger Painting

Figure 74 illustrates a painting by the twentieth century artist P'u Hsin-yü. Next to a tree by a river cavort two water buffaloes. Take a closer look and you will notice that these two small-sized beasts were not entirely painted with a brush. Their oval bodies are the imprints of P'u Hsin-yü's thumb, which was first lightly rolled in ink. In a previous chapter orthodox painting techniques were introduced, but that is not to say that only those paintings made with a brush count as Chinese painting. Like this painting of two water buffaloes, which is full of interest and atmosphere—its successful expression is the result of a great master's use of a playful method, one that relies on ink as opposed to brush. There are many examples of this kind of ink-expression throughout history. One of the most famous was the Ch'ing dynasty painter Kao Ch'i-p'ei, who often used his fingernails to paint. "Parrot" (fig. 75) is an example of his finger-painting. Kao Ch'i-p'ei's unorthodox method was clearly no impediment to the realization of a wonderfully lively image.

75 Kao Chi-pei, Ch'ing dynasty: Parrot.

2. The Mi Family Ink-play

Perhaps the most famous painter recorded as having practiced painting with unorthodox tools was Mi Fu of the late Northern Sung period. In place of a brush, he is said to have used half-eaten sugar cane and lotus pods. These would be used for the application of rough patterns of ink, to which details would later be added. This kind of performance became known as the Mi family ink-play. No doubt, interesting effects resulted from this innovative approach.

3. Lacquer Painting

Unusual painting techniques appear as early in Chinese history as

Left
73 Wu Ch'ang-shih, 20th century: Peonies.

the Chou and Ch'in dynasties. The following story is recorded in the early text *Han Fei-tzu*:

> There was a retainer who painted a pair of chopsticks for the Lord of Chou. It took him three years to complete. When the Lord saw that it was no different in appearance than any other lacquered chopsticks, he became angry. The painter of the chopsticks said: "Build a wall ten planks high and make a window eight feet in breadth. The moment when the sun first rises, place the chopsticks upon it and have a look." The Lord of Chou did as he was told and discovered dragons, serpents, birds, beasts and chariots, each one complete in form, all within the chopsticks. The Lord of Chou was delighted.

Unfortunately, these extraordinary lacquer chopsticks are long gone. Only oil-based pigments are used with lacquer and these, of course, differ fundamentally from the water-soluble pigments of ink painting. From the description in *Han Fei-tzu* we know that these particular chopsticks had to be seen from a particular vantage under light before the painted images would appear. This would seem to suggest a study of optics behind the making of these pieces, which in turn surprisingly suggests some points in common with the Op art that flourished in America during the 1960s.

4. Splattered Ink

The technique known as "splattered ink" also has a long history in China. Its origins can be traced back to Wang Mo ("Ink Wang," also called Wang Hsia) of the T'ang dynasty. His painting is described by the ninth century author Chu Ching-hsüan in *Record of Famous Paintings of the T'ang Dynasty*:

> No one knows where Ink Wang came from, nor his real name. He excelled at splattering ink to make landscape paintings and this is why people of the time called him Ink Wang. Oftentimes he would wander the lakes and rivers and it was his wont to paint landscapes with rocks, pines and other trees. By nature he was coarse and untamed and he was fond of wine. After a bout of drinking, he would splatter the ink. Laughing and chanting, feet rubbing, hands smearing, flinging it, pulling it, here pale, there jet-black—he would then follow the resulting configurations to make mountains, rocks, clouds and water. Answering his hands, following his inclinations, it was just like Creation itself. Sketching out clouds and mist, drawing out wind and rain from his ink washes, it was no different from divine skill. Most amazing of all, even a close inspection would not reveal the traces of his random ink splattering. Everyone described it as rare and different.

Chu Ching-hsüan's description makes the reader long to watch Wang Mo in action, to see that wine-inspired afflatus rise up and given form in his daubing and smearing. Here was painting that seems to have broken all known conventions of brush and ink. Alas, over a thousand year separate us from Ink Wang and all traces of his wild art are lost. We can, however, witness splattered ink painting of our own time in the work of Chang Dai-chien (1899-1983). Holding a bowl of ink with his hands, he would splatter it about the paper and from this jumbled mess bring forth a scene, like the legendary creator P'an Ku taking his ax to the undifferentiated chaos. This is the true skill of the splattered ink method.

5. Daubing with Ink—Washing the Silk

One aspect of painting to which the Chinese artist pays particular attention is the use of ink. Naturally, it is important for the artist to first acquire good quality ink. Then there are the limitless variations of tone that are possible, from lacquer-black to the slightest hint of pale tinted water. There are also various techniques in the application of layers and washes. If it is depth that is sought, then the painter applies a number of overlapping layers. If lightness is the goal, then after the painting is completed one can use the old method for cleaning clothes to wash the ink to the desired tone. This is described in Ho Yüan's miscellany of Sung dynasty date, *Ch'un-chu chi-wen*:

> When Chu Hsiang-hsien (active ca. 1094-1100) was young, he often despaired the fact that his paintings did not have the allure of depth and distance that one saw in the works of earlier painters. One day he casually painted a small mountain scene on a piece of Goose Spring silk. Unsatisfied, he hurriedly scrubbed away the old ink traces (as best he could) and three more times applied ink. Suddenly he realized he had something. After this, whenever he painted, Chu Hsiang-hsien would wash away the old ink. Otherwise, he would use a fine-textured stone to rub the painted silk. His intention was to make the ink enter deeply into the silk fibers.

The goal at first was simply to save a piece of silk. By accident, a new technique was discovered. Chu Hsiang-hsien's paintings are no longer extant, but judging from this description of washing away the ink, he was able to realize a certain beauty of the ambiguity of form and atmosphere. Ink, of course, is applied to the surface of the silk, while the painter concentrates on composition and appropriate tonal relationships. Chu Hsiang-hsien's use of something like pumice to rub the silk of the finished painting so that the ink would enter into the fibers of the silk is a supplementary technique designed to affect the painting's overall appearance.

6. Mixing Ink—Deep Indigo, Rattan Yellow, Dark Blue and Glue

Regardless of subject, the Chinese painter always seeks to infuse his ink with a transcendent, animated spirit and glow. Adding deep indigo (*ch'ing-tai*) is one particular method used by the painter. It is already described in Kuo Hsi's text on landscape painting, *Lofty Aspirations among Forests and Streams*. Kuo Hsi's painting "Early Spring" (figs. 10, 13) was painted in the fifth year of the Hsi-ning reign of Emperor Shen-tsung (1072), well over nine hundred years ago, yet the painting's ink tones remain startlingly vivid. Perhaps Kuo Hsi's method of mixing deep indigo with his ink had something to do with it; it is hard to tell today. From early texts, we also read of the use of rattan yellow (*t'eng-huang*. see p.56) together with ink. This is a technique promoted by the Yüan dynasty landscape painter Huang Kung-wang. He writes in his text *The Secrets of Landscape*: "To capture the subtlety of painting rocks, add to your ink-brush a wash of rattan yellow. This will naturally impart a richness of tone. But do not use too much; otherwise it will become difficult to move the brush. One can also get marvelous effects by occasionally adding dark blue

76 Hsü Wei, Ming dynasty: Peonies (detail from a scroll of flowers).

(*lei-ch'ing*)." By naked eye alone it is difficult to tell if Huang Kung-wang added rattan yellow or dark blue to the ink-work of such paintings as "Dwelling in the Fu-ch'un Mountains" (figs. 17, 122) or "The Nine Pearl Verdant Peaks." If one wishes to make ink deep and lustrous, one can also add a bit of glue dissolved in water. This is particularly well-suited for broad, carefree sketching done on rice paper (*hsüan-chih*). On unsized, absorbent *hsüan* paper each movement of the brush leaves its trace. Adding a touch of glue to the ink reduces this effect. This method is used in particular when applying washes. One painter who was especially fond of adding glue to his ink was Hsü Wei of the Ming dynasty. A detail of peonies from a long scroll of flowers (figs. 76) in a Japanese collection illustrates his skill with this technique. The ink has a crystalline clarity and richness which directly owe to the adding of a few drops of dissolved glue to the ink, as well as Hsü Wei's many years of experience and experimentation.

7. Licking the Brush

Although ink is a painting material, in the past, there were those who were exceedingly fond of it. Lu Hsing-fu of the Sung dynasty, for example, was so famous for his collection of ink that he was called ink-mad. In addition to collecting ink, there were those who liked to taste it. In fact, there is a phrase that describes painters raising the brush to "moisten the hairs with lips and suck the ink." In all likelihood this refers to two situations. The first is using one's mouth to suck out excess water from a brush yet uncharged with ink or pigment that will be used to apply a wash. The second situation pertains to painters of figures in the fine, meticulous style called *kung-pi*. For the details of face and hair, it is necessary to make the brush-tip exceedingly sharp. This can be achieved by drawing the brush through one's pursed lips. Doing so adds a touch of saliva to one's ink, which makes the consistency just right for this kind of painting.

8. Sprinkling

Innovative techniques allow the expression of new ideas. Two more examples beyond the confines of the usual are "sprinkling," which concerns the application of pigments, and the method of using rubbings. According to Wang Chia's *Shih-i chi*, in the first year of the reign of Ch'in Shih-huang-ti (246 B.C.), a foreigner named Lieh I from the far western regions possessed the remarkable talent of using his mouth to paint. Pigments were spit directly from his mouth, and all manner of strange beast would then appear. Sprinkling white pigment is commonly used for the painting of snow scenes. The most celebrated instance was the Yüan painter Wang Meng's painting of Mount T'ai in a blizzard. There are many records of this painting, but unfortunately the scroll itself is gone. It had been passed down through various collectors' hands in the Ming dynasty to Yao Kung-shou of Chia-hsing , in whose keeping Wang Meng's snowstorm was destroyed by a fire. For examples of this technique of sprinkling white pigment to suggest falling snow, we can look today at such paintings as "Travelers along the River in the First Snow" (fig. 77) by the Five Dynasties Period painter Chao Kan, "Fisherman in Snow" by an anonymous T'ang dynasty artist and "Dawn Snow in the Mountains" by the Southern Sung painter Hsia Kuei.

77 Chao Kan, Five dynasties period: Travelers along the River in the First Snow.

9. Rubbings

The use of rubbings in one's painting is a method seen in relatively recent times. This produces a very particular effect, at once antiquarian and awkward. A painting of peonies by the late Ch'ing-Republican Period artist Wu Ch'ang-shih (1844-1927) provides an illustration (fig. 73). The beauty of the rubbing is that it at once seems as heavy as the bronze ritual vessel from which it was taken, and as light as a cicada's wing. This kind of painting, espousing the antiquarian's aesthetic, appeals to the taste of the traditional collector. Rubbings for painting, however, need not be limited to ancient bronze vessels. There is an anecdote told of the Ch'ing dynasty painter Hsieh I-su (1811-64), who resided in Taiwan. He once mixed some red and white pigments and applied them directly to his backside. He sat on a piece of paper, producing a bum-dappled design, and then added a few leaves and branches. The result was a painting titled "Immortal Peaches."

10. Playing with Surface

There are no limits of bizarreness to a possible painting technique. Kuo Hsi, for example, promoted one called "looting the mud of the wall." He would take advantage of the natural concavities and convexities of a mud wall's surface and employ these in a landscape painted directly on the wall. The result, half-painting, half-sculpture, suggested the world's own creation. In mural painting, one often sees long brushstrokes that stand out from the surface. There is a term for this technique: "piled gold and standing powder." In principle, what one sees is not dissimilar to writing on a birthday cake: squeezed out of a confectioner bag, the colored icing leaves a long and well-rounded upraised line.

Under normal circumstances, painting surfaces are flat and two-dimensional. Raised or modeled strokes like these are simply intended to catch the eye, to add a new dimension to the painting. The most famous example of this, perhaps, is the Sung emperor Hui-tsung's painting of birds. Teng Ch'un describes it in his text *Hua chi*: "Oftentimes lacquer would be used for dotting the eyes. The effect was subtle—the dots no bigger than a small bean. Raised off the surface of the paper or silk, it would give the bird a remarkably life-like appearance. This was something others could not achieve." Teng Ch'un's description is confirmed by the painting "Bamboo and Finches" in the Metropolitan Museum of Art (fig. 78). The two birds in Hui-tsung's painting have eyes of beaded lacquer.

It is said that playing with techniques and methods is something anyone is capable of doing, but the ability to do it well varies from individual to individual. The subtle beauty of a transformed technique must stem from something deep within. Its purpose is to express the artist's ideas. From textual records, we learn of numerous other strange techniques. For example, there is "water painting," in which pigments floated on water are absorbed by paper and "fire painting," in which a burning piece of incense is used to puncture the paper.... Some of these techniques eventually lead to the art of handicrafts. As such, it is better that they be described elsewhere.

78 Emperor Hui-tsung, Sung dynasty: Bamboo and Finches.

Chapter Ten
Authenticating Paintings
Copies and Forgeries

The problem of "genuine" and "fake" paintings is also an intriguing topic in the Chinese tradition. Oftentimes one will find a seal on a painting that reads *mou-mou chien-shang*, "appreciated and examined by so-and-so." The last character, *shang*, or "appreciation," suggests the pure aesthetic enjoyment that accompanies viewing. This is a first step. Next one judges a painting's visual character and quality. Beyond that are questions of period style and authorship. All of this describes *chien*, "examination" or "discernment." These two characters, *chien* and *shang*, commonly appear together, but in fact they refer to two different stages of the process of examining a painting. When discussion of the basic principles regarding the appreciation and discernment of Chinese painting is finished, one can then talk about the making of fake paintings in traditional China.

"Fake paintings" by itself proves to be a rather broad topic, including two sub-categories of less-than-genuine paintings: the copy and the forgery. Paintings are not the same as paper currency. No one recognizes a counterfeit bill as money. When it comes to, say, a Ming dynasty scroll that is being passed off as Sung, however, while it may be wrong from the perspective of Sung dynasty art, it is certainly genuine from the standpoint of the Ming artist who painted it. The painting simply has to be returned to its proper context. This is even more the case with those paintings whose spurious signatures or labels are no fault of the artists who painted them, but rather the dirty work of later meddlers. There are two different categories of paintings which are wrongly attributed to an earlier artist. One type is the copy, the model of which is still known. The other type is the forgery, deliberately created as a fake from the beginning with the intention of deception. Of course, with respect to the painter whose name is on the label, both types of painting are "fake."

1. Examples of Copies

Copying paintings was a necessary practice in ancient times. Before photographic reproduction was possible, if a collector or artist owned a good painting and wished to share it with friends, the only way to do so, short of parting with his or her treasure, was to call in a professional painter to make a copy. In the National Palace Museum today, there is a letter written by the Northern Sung scholar Su Shih which reflects upon this common practice:

> One night I was looking for Huang Chü-ts'ai's "Dragon" but couldn't find it. Then I remembered that two weeks earlier Ts'ao Kuang-chou had borrowed it to have a copy made. It will be another month or two before I can get it back.

Su Shih, the owner of this earlier painting, certainly did not have the intention of making a fake. Rather, it was simply a matter of a friend borrowing it to have a copy made for his own study or enjoyment. We learn from this letter that the whole process of making a copy may take up to two months. While this in part can be attributed to the inconvenience of travel and communications in traditional China, the making of a copy was something that took time, especially if the professional copyist was taking pains to make the second version as accurate as possible. Of course, Su Shih and Ts'ao Kuang-chou would have had no problem telling apart the original Huang Chü-ts'ai from the copy, but with the passage of time this task becomes both more complicated and difficult.

The making of copies began much earlier than the Sung dynasty. Already in the Eastern Tsin, the great painter Ku K'ai-chih wrote about the techniques of copying other paintings. Moreover, the last of Hsieh Ho's Six Laws is specifically about copying: "Transmission is accomplished through the making of copies." This clearly reveals that the copying of earlier artists' work was an essential skill for learning how to paint. Great painters throughout the dynasties all copied earlier paintings, including Chao Meng-fu and the Four Great Masters of the Yüan dynasty. And right to the present day, anyone intent on learning the techniques of traditional Chinese painting cannot avoid this practice of copying. At first one may be copying the work of one's own teacher; eventually one moves on to the work of earlier painters. On top of this, professional ateliers of earlier times often passed down through their students models and copybooks. Time passes and later generations are left with a number of related versions of a single painting. The question of which is right and which is wrong naturally arises.

Probably the biggest case of a copyist taking advantage of this practice to switch the fake for the genuine took place in the T'ang dynasty during the reign of Wu Tse-t'ien (r.690-705). Chang Yen-yüan's *Record of Famous Paintings through History* includes the following account:

> During the reign of Empress Wu, Chang I-chih petitioned the court to summon painting craftsmen in order to repair paintings kept in the imperial treasury. Each of the craftsmen applied their skills according to their specialties. Exact copies were made and then refitted with the old mountings. There was not the slightest difference between the originals and the copies and quite a few of the genuine works ended up in Chang I-chih's hands.

Instances of people taking advantage of the process of copying to switch copies for originals occurred outside the court as well. Sometimes even the owner of the painting was fooled. Teng Ch'un recounts the following story in *A Continuation of the History of Painting*:

> During the Cheng-ho reign, there was a relative of one of the imperial concubines—his name is not known—who amassed a considerable collection of valuable paintings. Oftentimes other members of the imperial family would ask for his opinions concerning works of art, and over time, he consequently had frequent dealings with those who made a business of selling art. Whenever a rare work would come to his attention, he would use whatever crafty scheme available to get the

painting into his house. Accomplishing this, he would have an exact copy made and switch it for the original. The owner could never tell. Afterwards, he would sell the genuine painting for a high price. As this went on three or four times, people gave him the nickname Profit Times Three.

This kind of practice would not always succeed. One story of getting caught in the act is told of the Sung dynasty artist Mi Fu in a collection of anecdotes titled *A Grove of Records of Mi of Hsiang-yang*. A person approaches Mi Fu with the intention of selling a painting of a water buffalo by the famous T'ang dynasty artist Tai Sung. Mi Fu keeps the painting for a while, explaining that he wants to appreciate it for a few days before making his decision, and immediately puts to use his own considerable skill at making copies to produce an exact replica. Mi Fu gives the copy to the owner in place of the original painting, but the owner sees through Mi Fu's scheme because Tai Sung's original painting was so subtle that it included a reflection of the herdsboy in the eyes of the water buffalo—something Mi Fu had failed to notice. Regrettably, remarkable paintings like this are no longer seen.

Commonly, the process of copying is called *lin-mo* in Chinese, though in actuality, *lin* and *mo* refer to two different kinds of copies. *Lin* is the process of copying by sight from an original placed to the side. With this kind of copy, it is relatively easy to learn and duplicate the original's scale, tonal range of light and dark and overall configuration. However, it is difficult to avoid losing some likeness in the composition. For making a perfectly exact replica, one must use the *mo* process of copying, which consists of tracing the original onto a piece of paper or silk placed directly on top. This kind of copy follows every turn of the original brush, so that when placed side by side with the original, they look exactly alike. The problem, however, is that if one uses a rather heavy ink, it is easy for the ink to soak through the copy and stain the original. It is because of this that *ying-huang* or "hard yellow" tracing paper was invented. A yellow wax would be applied to thin paper and melted evenly across it with the use of a hot iron. The paper naturally becomes transparent. Moreover, the wax prevents the ink from seeping through and damaging the original painting or calligraphy that is being copied. Chang Yen-yüan had this to say: "Collectors are advised to always have on hand a ream of *hsüan* paper. With wax applied, one is then prepared to make copies. In earlier times this kind of exact copying was often done, with excellent results. Neither the spirit nor the precise traces of the brush would be lost." Another method sometimes used to help the copyist see the original as clearly as possible was to hold the painting, with paper or silk attached, up to a bright window and sketch the outlines. The Ch'ing collector and writer Chou Liang-kung writes in *Shu-ying tse lu* that in the T'ang dynasty, there were professionals specializing in copying calligraphy and they used custom-made tables with lamps built inside. This sounds much more comfortable than trying to copy while holding the source up to a bright window. Naturally, this table and method would be as effective for painting as it was for calligraphy.

2-1. Making Fakes

As for forgeries, the situation is even more complicated. "No sales for three years; one sale and you eat for three years." This old saying well describes the business of selling antiques. The difference in value between a genuine rare piece of art and a forgery is vast. Naturally, the unscrupulous will use every trick available to gain the enormous profit that comes with the successful selling of a fake, even setting traps. The simplest method is to get one's hands on a genuine work of art and make a copy. Wu Hsiu, in his *Lun-hua chüeh-chü* of the Ch'ing dynasty, records one instance of fakes being made that he witnessed himself:

> Kao K'o-kung's hanging scroll "Spring Clouds, Dawn Mists" is recorded in Kao Shih-ch'i's *Chiang-ts'un hsiao-hsia lu* (1693). During the Ch'ien-lung reign, Wang Yüeh-hsüan of Suchou purchased it from the Kao family of P'ing-hu for four hundred in gold. He then had a mounter surnamed Chang buy a half sheet of *ts'e-li* paper for five taels. This was split in two and made into two copies of Kao K'o-kung's painting by a man named Chai Yun-p'ing, whose fee was ten taels. For another ten taels, Cheng Hsüeh-ch'iao was hired to copy the signature and seals. The paintings were wet through with clear water and then plastered flat on a lacquer table. After the paintings were dry, the process was repeated as many as twenty or thirty times a day for three months. After that, the water of a boiled medicinal plant was applied to the paintings in order to remove the paper's luster. I saw for myself how this technique made the ink enter deeply into the fibers of the paper. The brushwork looked exactly like the original. The only thing slightly lacking was that profound sense of calm that one senses in Kao K'o-kung's painting; such divine resonance, in the end, eluded capture. One of the copies was provided with the original mounting of Kao K'o-kung's scroll, which included inscriptions by Wang Shih-min and Kao Shih-ch'i. Kao Shih-ch'i's original label was also added. At the time, Pi Chien-fei was convalescing from an illness and unable to leave his house. When he saw the painting, he sighed in admiration and bought it for eight hundred in gold. After recovering from his illness, he examined the painting more closely and realized that he had bought a fake, but nothing could be done. The second copy was also mounted. It was brought to Kiangsi Province where it fetched five hundred in gold from Ch'en Chung-ch'eng. Today the original is still in Suchou, but no one dares inquire of it.

From this story, we can see how a forger, with the investment of a mere twenty-five taels, could cheat his way to the vast sum of thirteen hundred in gold. It is worth noting how at this time the work of forging was already divided among different experts: one specialized in copying the painting, another the seals. On top of this, the owner of the painting adds to one copy the mounting of the original, replete with inscriptions and seals, which are precisely the things that encourage one's trust in a painting's authenticity. Dealers used to call this "the golden cicada molting its shell." Once the deal is struck, even if the new owner discovers that he has bought a fake, he has little choice but to keep quiet and swallow this bitter pill in order to save some face. Later he puts on his own act, showing off this magnificent "genuine" treasure, so as to cheat someone else.

The business of cheating can be quite involved—schemes devised by two or more people acting in tandem. Here is one example recorded by the Ch'ing dynasty author Lu Shih-hua in *Shu-hua shuo-ling*:

> Chang Chung's "Peach Blossoms and Mountain Birds" is a famous painting. Kao Shih-ch'i recorded it in *Chiang-ts'un hsiao-hsia lu*. In recent years, it was in a collection in Suchou. The owner was exceedingly fond of his treasure and he kept it hidden from sight. At the time there was a mounter in

Suchou who was exceedingly crafty. An official who was serving in that county was in the habit of passing his shop and praising the paintings that he saw there. The cunning mounter saw his chance and approached the owner of Chao Chung's painting. He told him that over time, the paste used for mounting would disintegrate, the paper would contract and the painting would be damaged every time it was unrolled. For this reason, it would be best to touch up the mounting. Once that was done, he would be advised to immediately store his painting safely away. This way he would not have to worry about his treasure. The owner believed him and entrusted Chao Chung's painting to him. The mounter thereupon hired someone to make a copy. Awaiting the visit of the art-loving official, the mounter hung the original Chao Chung high up on the wall. The official did eventually stop by and when he saw "Peach Blossoms and Mountain Birds," he asked how it came to pass that this painting had emerged from its collection. The mounter responded that the owner had grown tired of it and decided to get it remounted. Moreover, the owner would sell it for the original price he had paid. The official said that he knew what that price was and he definitely wanted the painting. The cunning mounter then responded, "But should I help in this transaction without any profit for myself?" The official agreed that the mounter should receive a commission and went home to get the money. The mounter thereupon switched the copy for the genuine, again setting it high on the wall. After a while, the official returned with the money. The mounter had already arranged matters with a servant from the household of the painting's owner, who pretended to take the payment for the painting. Meanwhile, the mounter collected his commission. The painting was then packaged up and handed over to the official. The original Chao Chung was later returned to its owner.

The famous twentieth century painter Ch'i Pai-shih had a seal that read, "My paintings roam the four corners of the world and among them half are fakes." Ch'i Pai-shih's reputation was far-reaching, so that even in his own lifetime forgeries of his work were filling the marketplace. But while the artist understood the situation, there was little he could do to protect the integrity of his work. Things were not the same as they are today, with copyright laws and litigation. Moreover, while calligraphy and painting can most certainly be treated as valuable commodities, in the past, these arts were foremost considered refined activities, removed from the dealings of the marketplace. Famous artists prided themselves on being idealistic and forgiving. Interestingly, one never hears of forgers being castigated by the original artists. In fact, not only does one never hear of any sanctioning or legal action being taken against a forger, to the contrary, what one mostly hears are sighs of admiration for his crafty skills. Naturally, this only encouraged the forgery industry. In an essay titled "Record of Mr. Shen Chou's Painting," the Ming dynasty calligrapher Chu Yun-ming writes of how extraordinarily popular Shen Chou's painting had become. As both cognoscenti and commoner actively sought his paintings, the opportunities for would-be forgers to see actual works increased markedly and fakes began to flood the market. If a genuine work appeared in the morning, a copy would follow by afternoon. Within ten days, a dozen or so versions would be floating around. The only way to judge authenticity was by examining the seals. With time, however, the seals that Shen Chou used also increased and the forgers became adept at imitating these as well. One then had to judge the paintings by the inscriptions, the same poems by Shen Chou appearing on all the different versions. Shen Chou, himself, never did anything to halt the forging of his paintings. To the contrary, he was proud of the fact that they had attracted such a wide audience.

2-2. The Substitute Painter

The imitation made by a substitute painter is yet another type of fake painting. Once a painter's reputation becomes established, requests for his work can multiply quickly. Overwhelmed by these commissions, the painter might ask one of his disciples to do the work for him. This, in fact, is a fairly common phenomenon. The painting may be done by the student, but with the master adding genuine signature, inscription and seals, it becomes especially easy to fool the customer.

Wu Hsiu, in *Lun-hua chüeh-chü*, mentions one instance of the substitute painter. Ch'en Chi-ju, friend of the famous painter Tung Ch'i-ch'ang (1555-1636), writes a letter to another painter named Shen Shih-ch'ung that reads, "I am having some white paper delivered to you, as well as three taels of 'brush-moistening' silver. I trouble you to do a large landscape, which I will need by tomorrow. Don't bother with a signature or inscription. I will want Tung Ch'i-ch'ang to add his name." Wu Hsiu then laments, "Today, fakes of Tung's paintings are everywhere; a good number of these are by Shen Shih-ch'ung and Chao Tso." Early in the Ch'ing dynasty, Chu I-tsun already warned would-be collectors of Tung Ch'i-ch'ang's work with the following words: "Chao Tso and the monk Hsüeh-k'o (Li Chao-heng) often helped Tung Ch'i-ch'ang when he was too busy to answer requests for his paintings. In the end, however, the waters of the Ching and Wei Rivers can be distinguished (an old allusion which reflects on connoisseurship) and those of the Tzu and Sheng, as well. One should beware of casually collecting simply because of the presence of Tung's inscription."

Substitute painters are particularly common with painters who also happen to be important government officials. Early in the Ch'ing dynasty, Chiang T'ing-hsi and Tsou I-kuei both had professional painters working for them. As for master-disciple relationships, Lo P'ing is well-known for painting in place of his teacher Chin Nung. It could also be a marital affair: Kuan Tao-sheng is said to have painted for her husband, Chao Meng-fu.

2-3. Other Methods of Forging Paintings

Another method of creating fakes was to meddle with old paintings that were already in hand. Most commonly, signatures and inscriptions would be erased and new ones would be added. An original inscription to the side could be trimmed off; one more to the center of a painting would have to be rubbed away. The signature of a well-known and measurably more salable painter would then be added. Almost always in such cases, a minor master's work would be reattributed to a more famous artist and a later work would be reassigned to an earlier dynasty. The reason why paintings by Tai Chin, the great Che school master of the early Ming, are so few is because quite a few of his paintings have already been changed to "Ma Yüans" and "Hsia Kueis" of the Southern Sung. Anonymous paintings, to begin with, have no authenticity problem, but unscrupulous dealers often take advantage of the missing signature and add one of a celebrated painter whose style of painting is relatively close. The painting of a white-robed scholar with a cane under some pine trees by an anonymous Sung dynasty painter illustrates this scenario (fig. 79). In the lower left corner are two characters

79 Anonymous, Sung dynasty: Walking with a Staff under Pines.

Tao-ning, but these must have been added by someone who knew relatively little about painting, for there is nothing in this painting to suggest the style of the Northern Sung painter Hsü Tao-ning. Far from it, this should be recognized as a fine little painting of the Southern Sung period. Chinese people love the antique, and in cases where signatures are added to anonymous paintings, it is often a matter of looking for a match somewhere in the distant past. Subject matter and style would be considered and then a name would be assigned. In the Sung dynasty this was already a common phenomenon: if the painting was a water buffalo, then the painting would be attributed to Tai Sung; if a horse, then it would be called Han Kan. According to painting histories, the Sung dynasty emperor Hui-tsung did a painting of a white eagle. Nowadays one sees examples of black eagles that are supposed to be from the imperial Hsüan-ho (Hui-tsung) brush.

Another method used in creating fakes is to assemble motifs copied from various different paintings by a single master. A tree might come from one painting, a rock from another and an inscription from yet another. In the end, everything more or less looks like this particular artist's style and a fake is born. Yet another form of fake concerns inscriptions. Inscriptions added to paintings are customarily written by the artist's friends or later collectors and appreciators and their content can range from aesthetic observations to more practical matters related to the artist and painting. In time, these inscriptions become a valuable source for art historians and connoisseurs alike. Inscriptions can help validate the authenticity of a given painting. This is where they become useful to the unscrupulous dealer, for the genuine inscription can be paired with a fake painting. A good, genuine painting is duplicated and then shorn of its original inscriptions, which are attached to the copy. Conversely, copies of the original inscription are added to the genuine painting. With genuine inscriptions, one is inclined to believe the painting, and if the painting is the original, who will then question the inscriptions? This method, which allows the dealer to kill two birds with one stone, is most amenable to handscrolls and album leaves, whose inscriptions are often mounted apart from the painting.

After the middle of the Ming dynasty, the region around Suchou became the center for painting in China and not a few specialists in forgery were active in this area as well. Chan Ching-feng, in *Tung-t'u hsüan-lan* (1591), many times describes problems related to the examination of paintings and calligraphy. In one case, even Wen Cheng-ming, the leading star of his generation, is fooled into buying a fake painting supposed to be by Shen Chou, who was Wen's own teacher. From this, one can understand just how skilled the forgers had become. By early in the Ch'ing dynasty, a street in Suchou named Chuan-chu Alley had become the center for the forgery industry. Ch'ien Yung, in *Lü-yüan hua-hsüeh*, describes a lively business in excellent fakes run by the Ch'in family, who lived on this street. According to Ch'ien, more than half of the attributions to famous painters of the Sung and Yüan dynasties, in all sizes and formats, came from the hands of this family. Then there were the Shen family twins, Lao-hung and Lao-ch'i, and Wu T'ing-li and Cheng Lao-hui, all of whom were expert at forging. All they needed was a chance to see a genuine painting. Within a few days, its exact replica would be ready. For calligraphy, these forgers would use the double-outline method, which consisted of carefully drawing the outlines of the strokes before filling the interiors. Paintings were just as carefully copied. In general, these Suchou fakes are known as "Suchou pieces." Most of them are painted in the fine-brush manner and are polychromatic. However, the range in quality is quite broad.

Other places in China were also known for their fakes. In Beijing, outside Ti-an-men Gate, was a man who specialized in forging works by the Italian painter at the Ch'ing dynasty court, Lang Shih-ning (Giuseppe Castiglione). Moreover, he owned a complete set of Ch'ing court seals, which he would impress on the paintings. There were two centers for the forging of the seventeenth century individualist Shih-t'ao, one in Canton and one in Yangchou. The Canton Shih-t'aos were often polychromatic, while the Yangchou Shih-t'aos commonly bore inscriptions written in large-sized cursive calligraphy with exaggerated diagonal strokes. Ch'ang-sha (Hunan) and K'ai-feng (Honan) fakes were largely created out of thin air. Nonetheless, the forgers' ability to make the paintings appear and smell antique was enough to take in some people.

Detail, **79**

3. Determining the Genuine from the Fake

The Yüan dynasty critic T'ang Hou wrote in *Ku-chin hua-chien* that in authenticating Six Dynasties Period paintings, one looks first at the silk and then at the brushwork. Authenticity, however, should always be based on the quality of the painting before anything else. To make a judgment on the basis of the silk first is putting the cart before the horse. T'ang Hou's recommendation is based on the principle that materials can help date a painting. After all, no Sung artist is going to use Ming dynasty silk, just as there is no way that a Ming edition of a Ch'ing dynasty dictionary can exist. Forgers, however, were not oblivious to this principle. They sometimes used old silk and paper to make their fakes. In such cases, anyone who looks only at the material upon which the painting was done will fall into the forger's trap. Of course, with time, it becomes harder and harder to get a hold of old paper and silk, but this would not stop the determined forger, who next turns to old publications for his source. One could remove the top and bottom of a Ming dynasty woodblock print, boil it to pulp and produce a small piece of new old paper. One could say that at this level, the forger's craft becomes a form of art by itself. The paper and silk of old paintings darkens in time. As described above in the case of forging Kao K'o-kung's "Spring Clouds, Dawn Mists," water made from boiling a medicinal plant could be used to remove the shine of the paper and make it appear older in age. More commonly, smoke would be applied to darken the surface, or leaking water would purposely be allowed to stain it and give the scroll the appearance of having been around for a long time.

In judging the authenticity of an old painting, one often finds old texts and catalogues to be quite useful. Over centuries of time in China, a number of books were written solely to record the transmission of important works of painting and calligraphy. Sung Hui-tsung's *Hsüan-ho hua-p'u* (1120) and the Ch'ing dynasty court's *Shih-ch'ü pao-chi* are examples of catalogues of the imperial collection. Such catalogues were also common outside the court. An Ch'i's *Mo-yüan hui-kuan* of the early Ch'ing is one example. If a painting is found to have been recorded in a catalogue such as these and thus known to have been in an imperial collection, or that of as discerning a connoisseur as An Ch'i, then the painting's provenance is to some degree established and its value goes up accordingly. In practice, many collectors place a lot of stock in these old catalogues. This allows the unscrupulous dealer yet another opportunity. During the Ch'ung-chen reign of the Ming dynasty, Chang T'ai-chieh published a book called *Pao-hui lu, A Record of Precious Paintings*. Included in this catalogue were paintings by famous painters dating all the way back to the Tsin and T'ang dynasties. After his book was in circulation for a few years, Chang had a number of fakes made, each one corresponding exactly to what he had recorded in his book, which consequently provided false confirmation of their authenticity. Here was a forger who was planning years ahead. A collector by the name of Kuan Mien-chun named his studio The Three Autumns Pavilion after three paintings by important early painters that he had managed to obtain: Yen Li-pen's "Autumn Cliffs, Returning Clouds," Huang Ch'üan's "Autumn Clarity on the Shu River," and Wang Shen's "Autumn Clouds of Ten-thousand Valleys." All of these were "precious paintings" from Chang T'ai-chieh's *Pao-hui lu*. Fakes from the late Ming are especially many.

We have now discussed the general circumstances surrounding the making of copies and forgeries. Let us now look at some examples of paintings that exist in more than one version. When placed side by side, it is not always difficult to judge the pearl from the fish eye.

Example 1: Ku Hung-chung's "The Night Revels of Han Hsi-tsai"

During the late years of his reign, Li Yü, the ruler of the Southern T'ang Kingdom of the Five Dynasties Period, was increasingly threatened by the emerging Sung dynasty to the north. Li Yü became extremely suspicious of the intentions of all subjects who had originally come from the north. This included Han Hsi-tsai, who hailed from Shantung Province. In order to protect himself, Han put on a show of extreme dissipation, pretending to be lost in women and wine and thus thoroughly disinterested in politics. Li Yü, ever distrustful, dispatched the professional painter Ku Hung-chung to Han Hsi-tsai's residence. In the era before the hidden spy camera, Li Yü ordered this court painter play the special role of photo-journalist: what Ku Hung-chung saw at Han Hsi-tsai's festivities was to be duly remembered and displayed in a painting. Ku Hung-chung's painting was a handscroll in five sections. The section illustrated here is the last one (fig. 80). The host of the party, Han Hsi-tsai, is shown standing and with left arm and palm raised, signifying who knows what to the seated guest and two lovely entertainers. Perhaps he does not wish to break the lovely dream his guests are living despite the lateness of the hour. Throughout the painting, the artist utilized the iron-wire brush-mode. His rendering of the weighty Han Hsi-tsai and guests, the long-sleeved maidens and interior furnishings, well confirms the remarkable descriptive powers of this important tenth century artist. Figure 81, which corresponds exactly to the section of the painting just described, is all that exists of another version of "The Night Revels of Han Hsi-tsai." Is the Beijing Palace Museum scroll (fig. 80) truly the original painting from the hand of Ku Hung-chung? Various early catalogues reveal that Ku's painting existed in at least three or four different versions. Some, in recent years, have argued that the landscapes depicted on the screens within the painting indicate a twelfth century style. Inscriptions following the painting begin with writers of the Yüan and Ming dynasties. In all likelihood, this is a Sung dynasty work. As for the fragment reproduced in Figure 81, we can simply quote the observation included in the National Palace Museum's catalogue *Ku-kung shu-hua lu*: "There are no seals or signature, but the painting is of great age. Although it is not Ku Hung-chung's original work, it is possibly a very early free-drawn copy."

Below
80 Ku Hung-chung, Five dynasties period: The Night Revels of Han Hsi-tsai. (Taipei Palace Museum collection)

Above
81 Ku Hung-chung, Five dynasties period: The Night Revels of Han Hsi-tsai (detail). (Beijing Palace Museum collection)

Example 2: Fan K'uan's "Travelers among Mountains and Streams"

The National Palace Museum alone has three different versions of Fan K'uan's famous landscape. Figure 82 is a detail of the original "Travelers among Mountains and Streams," which has already been introduced a number of times (see also Figures 6, 67). The painting is dominated by the great central massif, which is painstakingly built up with rain-drop texture strokes that allow the painter to approximate the geological characteristics of China's north mountains. Fan K'uan's painting also well evokes the dry climate of the T'ai-hang Mountain range. The country road, which dips slightly from right to left along the lower portion of the scene, establishes a horizontal balance to the uncompromisingly vertical orientation of the central mountain. Hidden among the leaves of the trees just above the heads of figures hurrying the pack animals along is Fan K'uan's signature. The painting is comprised of two pieces of silk sewn together, which is typical of large compositions of Northern Sung date. All of these things: style, hidden signature, format and above all quality, establish this painting as a genuine work. In fact, it is one of the great monuments of Chinese painting history, cited by everyone, doubted by no one.

The painting illustrated in Figure 83 carries a label that reads "Fan K'uan's 'Travelers,'" the same as Fan K'uan's masterpiece, minus the two characters "streams and mountains." Comparing the two, it becomes clear in an instant that this is a copy of Fan K'uan's original. How do we know this? For one thing, this version has little sense of the realistic flavor that typifies Northern Sung landscapes. Fan K'uan's original painting possesses a thundering strength that takes one's breath away. The imitation only follows the outer form. The main mountain has neither weight nor substance. Rather, one senses that the whole thing has been inflated with air, ready to float away as soon as the wind picks up. As for brushwork—whereas Fan K'uan's original "Travelers among Mountains and Streams" is largely painted with square, folding strokes, its copy utilizes a much rounder brushstroke. In the handling of the main peak, Fan K'uan elicits a natural progression in depth as one's eyes move from the center to the two sides. The copy possesses a limited sense of thickness, but beyond this, it has to rely on a layering effect to suggest depth. This is the difference between a painter who has experienced the landscape of "true mountains and true waters" and a copyist whose idea of landscape is limited to what appears on paper. If one looks at a copy of Fan K'uan's work by T'ang Tai, who was active during the K'ang-hsi reign of the Ch'ing dynasty, the stylistic features that appear in this copy and differentiate it from Fan K'uan's original are even clearer. For this reason, we surmise that this anonymous copy may well date to the late Ming.

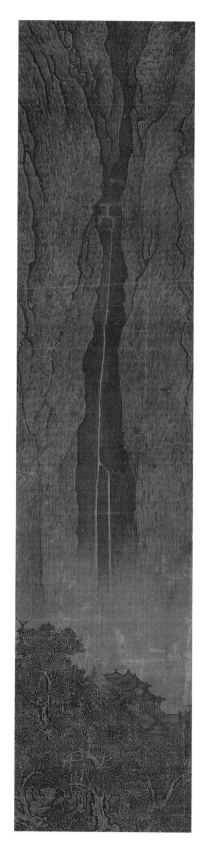

82 Fan K'uan, Sung dynasty:
Travelers among Mountains and Streams (detail).

Figure 84 reproduces a small-sized copy of Fan K'uan's "Travelers among Mountains and Streams." This is one leaf of a relatively large album of copies of landscapes titled "Tung Ch'i-ch'ang's Imitations of Sung and Yüan Paintings in Reduced Size." Four characters reading "To See the Big within the Small" provide a frontispiece and indicate the album's function as a model book of famous earlier compositions that were known in the early seventeenth century. The inscriptions are by Tung Ch'i-ch'ang; the paintings were possibly done by his younger contemporary, Wang Shih-min. As for this particular rendition of Fan K'uan's landscape, outside of an obvious shrinking of the main peak, one could call this a fairly faithful copy.

Left
83 Fan K'uan, Sung dynasty: Travelers.

Below
84 Anonymous, Ming dynasty: Reduced version of "Travelers among Mountains and Streams".

插篙菱渚繫艖艒
三更月上當篙頂老
漁爛醉喚不醒起來
霜印蓑衣影　唐寅畫

Example 3: T'ang Yin's "Drunken Fisherman among Reeds"

"Drunken Fisherman among Reeds" (fig. 85) presents a small corner of a river landscape. A small fishing boat is moored among the tall reeds. Under the thatched roof of the skiff, a fisherman is lost in sweet dreams, as he rests against the side of the boat. The fisherman's bamboo punting pole is seen on the other side; his coir jacket hangs from it. Gentle ripples stir the surface of the night river. A bright moon shines above. The painting is infused with an atmosphere that is at once peaceful and lonely. The artist's poetic inscription occupies a large portion of the painting's surface.

Precisely identical to "Drunken Fisherman among Reeds" is a painting titled "Moored Boat by the Reed Bank" (fig. 86). Not only is the composition exactly alike, the artist's inscription and signature too are an exact match, right down to the structures of the individual characters. When it comes to the quality of this painting, however, there is a notable difference: the ink tones are too heavy and the brushwork, especially of the sandy banks, is both stiff and jumbled. The calligraphy of the signature and inscription, too, gives the appearance of conscious copying. The brush lacks fluidity in the beginnings and endings of strokes, as well as in its general movements. There is little doubt that "Moored Boat by the Reed Bank" is a copy.

T'ang Yin's inscription:

Planted pole at the reed bank
    where the fishing skiff is tied;
At the midnight hour, the moon rises
    to the tip of the pole's reach.
The old fisherman in drunken sleep
    will not respond to calls;
By the time he arises, the print of frost
    will cover his jacket's shadow.

Left
85 T'ang Yin, Ming dynasty: Drunken Fisherman among Reeds.

Right
86 T'ang Yin, Ming dynasty: Moored Boat by the Reed Bank.

Example 4: Kuo Chung-shu's "Traveling along the River after Snow"

Kuo Chung-shu, a native of Loyang, Honan Province, is said to have been a person of unrestrained actions and personality. He was an accomplished man of letters who achieved renown as a calligrapher in the seal and clerical scripts and also as a painter. His birth and death dates have not been determined, but it is recorded that he served in office as a young man just prior to the establishment of the Sung dynasty in 960. During the reign of Sung T'ai-tsung, Kuo Chung-shu was awarded the position of Erudite of the National University, but because of his outspoken ways, he was demoted and eventually died out of favor.

Kuo Chung-shu's greatest achievements were accomplished as a painter of architectural subjects (*chieh-hua*. see Chapter 3.5). Ever since Ku K'ai-chih dismissed pavilions and terraced halls as objects of "fixed form" (and hence relatively simple to paint), architectural subjects were considered to be the concern of craftsmen. Relying on his considerable talents, however, Kuo Chung-shu was able to elevate this "lifeless" subject to a new plateau and help establish it as a viable subject for Chinese painting. After Kuo Chung-shu, many of the great painters of the Sung dynasty, including Yen Wen-kuei, Chao Po-chü, Wang Shen and Li Kung-lin, became skilled painters of architectural subjects.

The details of the two boats illustrated in Figure 87 are extraordinary. Hulls, cabins, rudders and masts are all depicted with a tightness and logic that is thoroughly convincing. In the upper left corner is a short inscription by the Northern Sung emperor Hui-tsung: "Kuo Chung-shu's 'Traveling along the River after Snow,' a genuine trace," followed by Hui-tsung's seal, "Treasure of imperial writing." The painting itself no longer carries the signature of Kuo Chung-shu, so we must rely on Hui-tsung's word for making the attribution. Looking at the painting, one notes that the two long ropes that extend right from the masts of the boats are cut off by the right border of the painting. Above is a poetic inscription by the Ch'ing dynasty emperor Ch'ien-lung, who comments on this: "When was it that this large

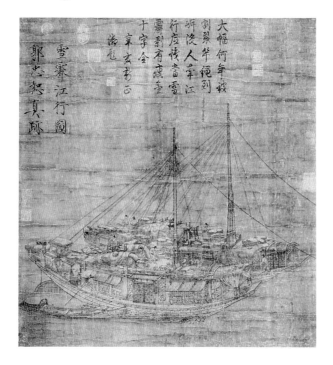

Left
87 Kuo Chung-shu, Sung dynasty: Traveling along the River after Snow. (Taipei Palace Museum collection)

Right
88 Kuo Chung-shu, Sung dynasty: Traveling along the River after Snow. (Nelson-Atkins Museum of Art collection)

scroll was cut? Bamboo cables reach to a shore where no one pulls."
Ch'ien-lung's determination that the painting had been cut at some time
was absolutely correct. This painting is mentioned in Chan Ching-feng's
Tung-t'u hsüan-lan:

> Kuo Chung-shu's "Traveling along the River after Snow." The landscape's
> texturing combines the "small hemp-fiber" and "scraped iron" brush-modes,
> which are derived from Wang Wei's "Waiting for the Tidal Bore." At the
> beginning of the scroll are layers of distant mountains and scattered trees,
> barely an inch tall. Mountains and trees well balance one another. Towards
> the end of the scroll is a ship, a foot in length. Tied to its back hull is a small
> boat, about four inches in length. A number of people are depicted on the
> shore at the beginning of the painting, pulling the boat upstream. Figures and
> the details of the boats are all depicted with meticulous attention and logic.

From this we know that a large portion of the painting's beginning is
missing, including the distant mountains, scattered trees and cables.
Possibly, this is the result of an unscrupulous dealer's attempts to gain
two sales from a single painting. By coincidence, the full composition of
this painting can still be seen in a copy now in the collection of the
Nelson-Atkins Museum in Kansas City (fig. 88). The Kansas City version
confirms that the original painting was a handscroll and that the content
was exactly as Chan Ching-feng described. When this copy was made and
by whom is not known, but there is no question that it is a copy: the
brushwork of both the painting and Hui-tsung's inscription is exceedingly
weak. The earliest seals that can be read from the painting belong to the late
Ming collector Hsiang Yüan-pien. Afterwards, the painting entered the
Ch'ing imperial collection. From this we determine that the copy was
probably made by the middle of the Ming dynasty.

The four examples presented here are fairly typical cases. Probably the
single most famous controversy concerning a copy centers on Huang
Kung-wang's "Dwelling in the Fu-ch'un Mountains," two versions of which
are in the National Palace Museum. In fact, which of these two scrolls is the
genuine item and which is the copy is a question still being argued today.
When it comes to determining the genuine from the fake, there is certainly
no substitute for special training. Nonetheless, there is also no question that
one must first have the ability to appreciate a painting before developing
the connoisseur's ability.

Chronology

Shang	c.1500-c.1050 B.C.
Western Chou	c.1050-771 B.C.
Eastern Chou	
Spring and Autumn Period	770-475 B.C.
Warring States Period	475-221 B.C.
Ch'in	221-207 B.C.
Han	
Western Han	206 B.C.-A.D.9
Hsin	9-25
Eastern Han	25-220
Three Kingdoms	
Shu	221-263
Wei	220-265
Wu	222-280
Six Dynasties Period	
Western Tsin	265-316
Eastern Tsin	317-420
Liu Sung	420-479
Southern Ch'i	479-502
Liang	502-557
Ch'en	557-589
Sui	589-618
T'ang	618-906
Five Dynasties Period	906-960
Sung	
Northern Sung	960-1127
Southern Sung	1127-1279
Chin	1115-1234
Yüan	1279-1368
Ming	1368-1644
Ch'ing	1644-1911

Part Two

An Introduction to the History of Chinese Pinting

Chapter One
The Ancient Period

89 Anonymous, Warring States Period (Ch'u): Female Shaman.

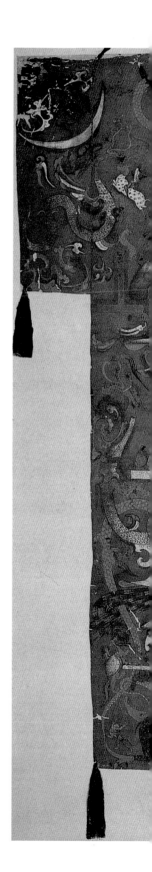

A vast gulf of time separates us from the paintings of China's early history, and consequently most of what once existed is unknown to us. Nonetheless, a few things can be understood from the designs and decorations that adorn various types of objects that have survived or been unearthed. During the Neolithic Period, the distant ancestors to the Chinese people were already painting images and designs on earthenware pots. These lively patterns painted with a brush have a generous and open air. The special attraction of the brush-and-ink tradition, with its emphasis on line, would eventually form the foundation for Chinese painting. During the Shang dynasty, bronze ritual vessels were cast with a variety of decorative patterns, including the *t'ao-t'ieh* animal mask. Various methods of formal organization or aesthetic principles such as balance, symmetry, repetition and scale are revealed in these designs. The designs on bronze ritual vessels of the Spring and Autumn Period and Warring States Period of the Eastern Chou include representational scenes with figures, animals and mythical creatures. From these we can surmise that the art of painting had already attained a certain level of artistry.

The earliest known painting on silk was unearthed from a tomb of the region known in ancient times as Ch'u, near Ch'ang-sha in Hunan Province (fig. 89). It dates to the fourth or third century, B.C. A slim-waisted woman is depicted standing and in profile, her long robe reaching to the ground. Her two hands are brought together in front of her in what appears to be a kind of formal greeting or supplication. Dancing above her head is a large phoenix which seems to be depicted in the middle of a struggle with a *k'uei* dragon. The lines in

126

90 Anonymous, Han dynasty: Banner from Ma-wang-tui.

the painting are quite animated, as is the description of the phoenix's struggle with the serpent. The woman is given a graceful, regal bearing. This, in particular, demonstrates a certain skill of representational drawing on the part of the painter.

1. The Han Dynasty

The imperial kingdom of the Han dynasty was powerful and magnificent. The arts flourished. Professional painters were employed to serve at the court, which also instituted the practice of collecting famous works of painting and calligraphy. At this time, paintings were used on a broad scale for the didactic purpose of spreading moral lessons among the people. The famous ninth century art historian Chang Yen-yüan spoke of the early development of painting in China. He considered that by the Ch'in and Han dynasties, painting had already reached a level of relative maturity, but he lamented the fact that the products of this early period could no longer be seen. The situation is not quite as dismal as it was a thousand years ago. Archaeological work has uncovered quite a number of Han dynasty tombs with mural paintings, so we have actually more opportunities to see Han painting than Chang Yen-yüan.

Certainly, the most prominent example of Han dynasty painting to be discovered to date is the silk banner unearthed in 1972 from the tomb of the noblewoman Tai (fig. 90) at Ma-wang-tui, near Ch'ang-sha. It was made circa 193-186 B.C. and draped over her innermost coffin. The painting, which is in the shape of a 'T', divides into three portions that signify heaven, the human realm and the underworld. At the right of the upper portion is the sun, within which is a golden bird. Below it is depicted the mythical Fu-sang tree, which was believed to hold nine suns of its own. A crescent moon is seen at the upper left along with the toad and hare that were associated with it. Ch'ang-o, the goddess of the moon, is seen charging towards it, carrying with her the elixir of life. At the center of the upper portion is the image of a woman with a serpent's body. The central portion of the banner is the most important. An elderly woman is portrayed leaning forward on a cane. Two attendants kneel in front of her; three are standing behind her. The painting here, which is especially fluid, should be considered one of the great works of Han dynasty figure painting. The lower portion of the banner describes an underwater world of strange creatures. A giant man standing on the bodies of two large serpents is shown at the very bottom. In the central and lower portions, one finds two coiling dragons, their bodies penetrating through the center of a jade *pi* disk. Also seen are snakes, tortoises, birds with human heads, bats and strange beasts. From an art historical perspective, one must acknowledge that the anonymous painter who made this banner was extremely skilled at putting together a composition. Heaven, earth and the realm of man are artfully combined to describe the Chinese universe, along with the realism of human affairs and the imagination of the spirit world.

Han dynasty mural paintings have been found at Wang-tu in Hopei Province, Ho-lin-ko-erh in Inner Mongolia and Loyang. Figures remain the primary subjects of these paintings and they are done in a variety of styles, but no matter whether that style is elegant, awkward or unconventionally loose, in each case the painter was able to use his brush to capture the vitality and spirit of his subjects.

Painting-related representational art of the Han dynasty can also be seen on molded bricks and in stone engravings which were used to decorate tombs. While such tombs have been found throughout the country, the highest concentrations are in the provinces of Shantung, Ssuchuan and Honan. Before the carving of the stone could take place, there would have to be a sketch, as one would have for painting. These can thus be seen as reflections of painting of the time. The most outstanding of the Han stone engravings were found in the Wu Liang and Hsiao-t'ang shrines in Shantung Province. The figures are portrayed in a strong, severe style full of antique flavor. As for the molded bricks discovered in Ssuchuan, these include remarkable portrayals of daily activities, all brought to life with strong, abbreviated lines.

From the painted designs on Neolithic pots, the Warring States description of the standing maiden, as well as from the Western Han banner and mural paintings from Ma-wang-tui, it can be seen that the art of linear description that would later serve as the foundation of the Chinese painting tradition is already well established. Moreover, the images on molded bricks and engraved stone, while technically close to light relief carving, also predominantly rely upon the line for expression. Whether it is a painting on a wall, on silk, or an inlaid pattern in bronze, linear expression in this early period already reveals itself to be multi-faceted. As for the use of colors , it appears

91 Ku K'ai-chih, Tsin dynasty: Admonitions of the Court Instructress (detail).

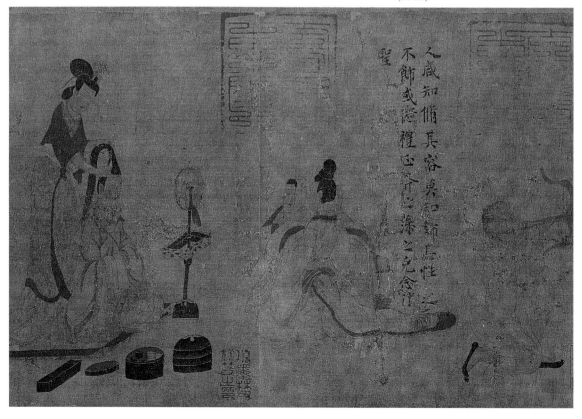

that black and red were the primary pigments.

Figures remained the dominant subject of painting during the Han and Tsin dynasties. Late in the Eastern Han period, Buddhism entered China and with the religion came the need to establish temples and forge images. As Buddhism gained popularity, Buddhist painting also flourished, especially for decorating temples. During the Three Kingdoms Period (221-80) immediately after the Han, Ts'ao Pu-hsing of Wu gained a reputation for his skill in describing the Buddhist images of the Western regions. Stylistically and technically important changes took place during this period that were largely due to the influence of Buddhist art. The simplified, blunt and antique modes of description found in Han painting evolved towards a finer, denser style. Wei Hsieh was influenced by Ts'ao Pu-hsing and produced paintings that were extremely fine with tight, intricate compositions.

2. The Six Dynasties Period

Early in the fourth century, foreign tribes living on the borders of China forced the ruling court of the Tsin dynasty to flee east. With this change in political fortunes, the center of Chinese culture also shifted from the Yellow River region to the Yangtze River basin. Although the Eastern Tsin was limited in geographic scope, culturally it produced one of the greatest phases in all of Chinese history.

Living at this time was the great painter Ku K'ai-chih (ca. 344-406) who also proved to be a discerning commentator on painting. His texts include *A Critique of Painting*, which provides discussion of paintings from the Wei and Tsin periods, and *A Record of Painting Cloud-Terrace Mountain*, which is a detailed discussion of the methods involved in one painting. Although difficult to read and understand, these writings have provided later generations with a glimpse of the painting theory and techniques of this early period. Ku K'ai-chih wrote of "moving one's thought to gain the marvelous," which refers to the necessity of the painter to understand the intrinsic qualities and emotions of his subject and the importance of giving them form in one's painting. Happily, an important attribution to Ku K'ai-chih has survived to our time. This is "Admonitions of the Court Instructress" (figs. 8, 30, 91) which is now in the collection of the British Museum. Many consider this painting to be a later copy, but it nonetheless preserves the style and art of Ku K'ai-chih. The painting is on silk with light colors applied. The figures, whose countenances are at once solemn and tranquil, are described with a thin, unmodulated brush-line. The most striking feature of the scroll is the linear expression of the clothing folds. Equally impressive is the tight, interactive arrangement of figures. The brush-mode of Ku K'ai-chih's painting has been described as "spring silkworms spitting silk." The special characteristic of this mode is that it at first appears thoroughly placid and of little interest. The longer one looks, however, the more one senses a ceaseless, underlying rhythm that generates energy throughout the painting. Unwittingly, the viewer is caught in this energy and carried away with a light, floating sensation. In Ku K'ai-chih's hands, the ancient style of Chinese dress with long hanging robes is rendered masterfully. Limitless variations of weight and form are suggested by his smoothly flowing brush. In comparison to the female shaman seen in the Warring States Period cloth painting, Ku K'ai-chih's figures demonstrate the painter's movement towards more complex, tightly meshed compositions.

During the Eastern Tsin and the ensuing Six Dynasties Period, discussions of abstruse philosophical principles flourished and there was an active pursuit of an elegant, natural life-style. In this atmosphere, scholars and aristocrats alike became increasingly interested in painting as an art. This was also a period of frequent warfare and political treachery. With danger and disaster never far, those of pure mind and aspiration often secluded themselves in the relative tranquillity of mountains and forests, accompanied by mists, streams and rocks. This helped generate the first sprouts of landscape painting.

Among the early landscape painters were Tsung Ping and Wang Wei, who sketched the scenery they had seen during personal sojourns through the mountains. The two also authored texts on landscape painting. Tsung Ping's *Preface to Landscape Painting*, while quite short, helps establish the value of landscape painting. He describes the methods of landscape depiction—reducing in size the scenery of the natural world while maintaining a proper sense of scale. He also speaks of being sympathetic to the subtleties of nature and of being able to use these to move the viewer's heart and establish rapport with the divine thoughts of sages of the past. Tsung Ping's contemporary, Wang Wei, wrote a text titled *On Painting* in which he talks of using different modes of brush-description to capture the complexities and ever-changing phenomena of nature. The painter's landscape is an emotional reaction to what he sees and a projection of his own spirit: "Gazing towards autumn clouds, one's spirit rises with the wind; caressed by the spring wind, one's thoughts become wide and expansive." After these two artists, landscape painting began to move away from figure painting and establish itself as an independent subject.

Lu T'an-wei, Chang Seng-yu and Ku K'ai-chih are recognized as the three great masters of the Six Dynasties Period. Lu T'an-wei was

92 Anonymous, Six dynasties period: Seven Sages of the Bamboo Grove (detail).

the most trusted painter of the court of Emperor Ming-ti during the (Liu) Sung dynasty. He is said to have been an excellent figure painter, one especially skilled in Buddhist subjects. He also painted images of the sages of antiquity. His brushwork is described as being tensile and sharp; his brush was likened to a sharp, singing blade. The figures it produced were life-like and animated beyond any common standard. Like Lu T'an-wei, Chang Seng-yu was a native of Wu (modern-day Suchou) and he was also adept at using the calligrapher's brush methods to paint. One special characteristic of Chang Seng-yu's painting, according to textual descriptions, was the skillful use of shadows to highlight the figures and objects. This gave his paintings a three-dimensional quality that people of the time considered highly unusual. Scholars today presume that the technique came from India. If so, it would be one example of foreign influence on Chinese painting.

During the Six Dynasties Period, China was divided between the north and the south, and the styles of the two regions differed. With the unification of the country under the Sui, the different styles gradually moved towards integration.

3. Hsieh Ho's Six Laws

1. Breath-resonance,
      generated by movement.
2. Bone-method,
      from the use of the brush.
3. Responding to the object,
      by depicting its form.
4. According with kind,
      by the application of color.
5. Organizing and planning,
    by the disposition of elements.
6. Transmitting and transplanting,
      by making copies.

It has already been mentioned that Ku K'ai-chih authored texts on painting. There were others before him who also touched upon aspects of this art. In *Han Fei-tzu*, for example, it is argued that dogs and horses—things that everyone has seen—are more difficult to paint than ghosts and demons. In *Chuang-tzu*, there is a brief reference to the painter who unceremoniously loosened his clothes and squatted on the floor—an expression of his unconventionality. These, however, are limited examples. Fuller expositions on the art of painting do not emerge until the Eastern Tsin and Six Dynasties Period, and of these the most famous is certainly Hsieh Ho's *Evaluating Ancient Paintings (Ku-hua lu)* of the mid-fifth century. Included in this work is the celebrated Six Laws of Painting, which opened a new horizon for painting theory in China. After Hsieh Ho, the Six Laws provided the foundation for both theory and practice for all later periods.

There have been numerous attempts over time to explain exactly what the Six Laws mean. We limit ourselves here to a very general explanation. "Breath-resonance, generated by movement" points to the issue of life and vitality in one's painting. "Bone-method, from the use of the brush" focuses on the significance of the brush-line and its importance for establishing the structure of the subject. "Responding to the subject, by depicting its form" simply refers to the accuracy of one's drawing which must follow the appearance of the subject. "According with kind, by the application of color" pertains to the issue of preserving the intrinsic character of the subject by rendering it with the colors appropriate to its genre. "Organizing and planning, by the disposition of elements" refers to composition, one of the essential elements in painting. "Transmitting and transplanting, by making copies" points to the process of reproducing images from one source to another, reducing and enlarging them to make one's painting complete.

Chapter Two
The Sui and T'ang Dynasties
589~906

1. The Golden Age of Figure Painting

The Sui and T'ang dynasties represent a glorious phase in the history of China, and in painting as well. It was a period of great achievements. While this was the golden age of Chinese figure painting, landscape and birds-and-flowers also earned the status of independent subjects.

The most famous painters of the short-lived Sui dynasty were Chan Tzu-ch'ien (ca. 550-604) and Tung Po-jen (active late sixth and early seventh centuries). Both painters exhibited remarkable breadth and expertise in painting architectural subjects, figures and landscapes. Chan Tzu-ch'ien hailed from Hopei; Tung Po-jen came from the Yangtze River region to the south. Both were summoned to the court where they met and mutually disdained each other's style. Nonetheless, over time, one adopted the other's strong points, and in this fashion the northern and southern styles eventually merged.

Figure painting developed magnificently in the T'ang dynasty. Among the Early T'ang painters, Yen Li-pen (ca. 601-73) is generally considered the most important. Judging from "The Emperors" (fig. 93), a long handscroll that depicts thirteen emperors of earlier times and is associated with Yen Li-pen, the artist's descriptive line moved with slow, deliberate speed. This is an iron-wire brush-line with no modulation at all. Red and black are the dominate colors. The figures well exhibit the pomp and gravity of the emperors' exalted positions. This is the fine-brush style of painting associated with the Early T'ang. The second prominent painter of the period was Wei-ch'ih I-seng (active late seventh century) who came to China from Central Asia. Wei-ch'ih I-seng was especially skilled as a painter of foreign and Buddhist subjects. According to textual accounts, his painting style also employed a fine, tensile brush-line. Described as being like coiled iron-thread, it possessed a transcendent energy which must have found accord with the Chinese painting style. Wei-ch'ih I-seng was also known for modeling the "ins and outs" of his subjects. This supports the idea that three-dimensionality in painting was introduced to China from India and Central Asia.

The High T'ang witnessed the emergence of one of China's greatest figure painters, perhaps the greatest of all time: Wu Tao-tzu (ca. 680-760). Wu Tao-tzu has been labeled the "sage of painting," and he has been considered the ancestral master to all professional painters who have come from the ranks of the common people. Already in his youth, he had attained a reputation in the capital Ch'ang-an for a style of painting that was bold and powerful. Chang Yen-yüan's *Li-tai ming-hua chi* records, "While others are still huddled in careful study, I, Wu Tao-tzu, am already dotting and

Left
93 Yen Li-pen, T'ang dynasty:
The Emperors (detail).

dashing. While others take pains to get the likeness just right, I, Wu Tao-tzu, transcend such common concerns." One discerns from this self-statement that beyond verisimilitude, Wu Tao-tzu filled his painting with a transcendent energy that left far behind the efforts of lesser painters. Another characteristic of Wu Tao-tzu's figure painting was that structure was entirely established by brush-lines; color was unnecessary. This simplified form of painting, called *pai-miao* or "plain drawing," later would be made famous by Li Kung-lin during the Northern Sung. Its success was owed to the fact that linear drawing had, in Wu Tao-tzu's hands, attained a level of unmatched virtuosity. At this level of maturity, color was no longer needed. The power of Wu Tao-tzu's *pai-miao* painting is well illustrated by the story of the hell scene he painted in the capital. This so frightened the butchers and fish-mongers who saw it that they hastened to change their professions.

One of the early designations of figure painting in China is the "two styles of Ts'ao and Wu." Ts'ao refers to the Northern Ch'i painter Ts'ao Chung-ta, a specialist of Buddhist icons. He rendered clothing folds with dense, layered lines to suggest the clothing's snug wrapping. His subjects appeared to be wearing water-soaked gauze, which so tightly adhered to the body that it led some to describe it as "Ts'ao's robes emerging from water." One can perhaps picture the effect by looking at some of the early sculpture of the Yun-kang caves near Ta-t'ung (Shansi Province), which was strongly influenced by the Mathura style of sculpture of the Gupta period in India. In contrast, Wu Tao-tzu's brushwork was rounded and revolving, full of variations of speed and pressure. This gave his clothing the appearance of floating in air—"Wu's sash swept by the wind" as it was described. These two different styles reveal that by the T'ang dynasty, native brush-modes had joined with foreign influences to create a new style of painting.

The paintings of these celebrated masters can no longer be seen. Nonetheless, some idea of contemporary standards for figure painting can be gained by looking at the mural paintings that decorate the tomb of the imperial prince Li Chung-jun and were completed early in the eighth century (fig. 94).

94 Anonymous, T'ang dynasty: Maiden from the mural painting of the tomb of Li Chung-jung (detail).

2. The Transformation of Landscape Painting

During two hundred fifty years of the T'ang dynasty, figure painting evolved and dominated as an art of peerless accomplishment. Following the development of figure painting, however, the art of landscape painting gradually matured, and by the end of the T'ang and into the ensuing Five Dynasties Period and Northern Sung, it supplanted figure painting as the dominant subject in Chinese painting. It would remain so through the later dynasties. This establishes a fundamental distinction with Western painting which continued to focus on the human figure. Before describing the historical development of Chinese landscape painting, it is worth considering why landscape comes to inhabit such an important place in Chinese art. Part of the answer can be traced back to certain currents in Chinese philosophy, but we must also consider the long-standing importance accorded to landscape in Chinese

95 Anonymous, T'ang dynasty: Landscape on a biwa plectrum guard (detail).

literature, which no doubt provided fertile ground for the later development of landscape painting.

To Confucius is ascribed the following observation: "The humane delight in mountains; the wise delight in water." Substantial and unmoving, mountains provide a fitting symbol for calm stillness. Ceaselessly flowing water, meanwhile, symbolizes movement. Mountains and water, *shan-shui* ("landscape"), thus collectively encompass all of nature. With a single brush, the skilled painter has the means to grasp the myriad transformations and subtleties of the universe. Figure painting cannot easily escape the strictures of narrative and didactic teachings, while birds and flowers remain small objects, easily observed and easily painted—a genre that will always present a limited piece of nature's big picture, especially in comparison to the grand view of landscape. Chinese intellectuals through history have largely exhibited two manners of thought: outwardly in their social roles they are Confucian, but inwardly they preserve the Taoist's commitment to self-cultivation. The Taoism of Lao-tzu and Chuang-tzu promotes a return to nature and the nurturing of the ideals of reclusion. The Chinese scholar lives in the mundane world, but he longs for the freedom of nature. Locked in the dusty strait-jacket of social affairs, he dreams of carefree whistling among rocks and streams. Unable to realize such dreams, his aspirations are entrusted to brush and ink, which allow the hidden mysteries of mountains and woods and the comings and goings of clouds and mist to be seen and experienced. Forged by these two dominant streams of thought, the Chinese attitude towards nature is precisely the opposite of what is found in the West. In the West, nature and humans are seen as two separate entities, often in opposition to one another. In China, the two can be united as one. After the Tsin court moved south in the fourth century, politics and society remained unsettled, and the lives of the intelligentsia lacked stability and security. Philosophical speculation on the mysteries of nature flourished, and many chose to live as hermits among mountains and forests. A landscape school of literature extolling the virtues of nature arose at this time. What could not be expressed in song and poem was entrusted to pictures: a place to lodge journeys that could be enjoyed while at rest.

Prior to the T'ang dynasty, there were those who earned repute for skill in depicting landscape, including Ku K'ai-chih, Tsung Ping, Wang Wei and Chan Tzu-ch'ien. However, true landscape painting did not emerge until the arrival of the High T'ang painters Li Ssu-hsün (653-718) and Wu Tao-tzu. Landscape painting gradually emerged from its earlier role as background to figure painting. It is true that one finds the label landscape painting prior to the High T'ang (ca. 680-760), but what existed at this time remained technically immature and limited. With the emergence of Li and Wu, landscape painting began to shed its second-class status. According to historical records, the following story took place with regard to landscape styles of these two artists. During the T'ien-pao reign (742-55) of Emperor Ming-huang, the emperor began to reminisce of the scenery of the Chia-ling region of Ssuchuan Province. He thereupon ordered Wu Tao-tzu to travel there in order to make a realistic painting of the area. After Wu returned, the emperor asked how his work was proceeding. Wu

Tao-tzu replied that he had no sketches; all sceneries were lodged in his memory. The emperor ordered him to paint it on a mural of the Ta-t'ung Palace and Wu Tao-tzu did as he was asked, depicting one hundred miles of the scenery of Chia-ling in a single day. At that time, Li Ssu-hsün was also well-known as a specialist of landscape painting and Ming-huang also requested him to paint the scenery of Chia-ling on the walls of the Ta-t'ung Palace. Li also finished the commission, but it took him a number of months. Both artists' work, according to the emperor's evaluation, were the height of excellence. The two expressions, "finished in one day" and "labored over many months," encapsulate the two schools of Chinese landscape painting that later develop: "fine brush" *(kung-pi)* and "sketching ideas" *(hsieh-i)*. Li Ssu-hsün was a member of the T'ang ruling family. His style of painting, derived from Chan Tzu-ch'ien, was characterized by strong, thin brushwork and glittering colors that included green and gold. This style of landscape painting later earned the label "blue-and-green." Wu Tao-tzu's linear style of "idea sketching" later led to an alternative approach to landscape depiction.

A later contemporary of these two artists was Wang Wei (701-61), whose style of landscape painting contrasted with the style of Li Ssu-hsün by virtue of use of inkwash instead of color. Prior to this period of the T'ang dynasty, Chinese painting, like Western painting, emphasized the use of colors, even if the concept of colors differed. Hsieh Ho, we are reminded, speaks of the use of colors in his Six Laws, but not of ink. After Wang Wei, however, the palette of Chinese painting largely becomes composed of ink's myriad tones. According to textual records, Wang Wei specialized in level distance scenes of landscape. Coiled mountains and valleys and flying clouds and waters all combined to produce landscapes with a distinctively poetic flavor. Wang Wei was a multi-talented artist. Besides earning fame as a painter, he was also known as a poet and musician. Later critics described his paintings as possessing poems and his poems as possessing paintings. His influence on later generations was profound.

3. Painting after the High T'ang

There were other artists similarly engaged with experiments in ink and inkwash, though with a different emphasis from Wang Wei. Two such figures were Chang Ts'ao and Wang Hsia (Wang Mo or "Ink Wang"). Chang Ts'ao is especially known for his famous comment, "Outwardly, I learn from the Creator; inwardly, I plumb the source of my heart," which has since become an oft-repeated maxim among painters. "Outwardly learning from the Creator" suggests the artist's reliance on the outside world of nature to provide the source for his or her inspiration . "Inwardly plumbing the source of one's heart" refers to the artist's ability to transfer his or her own thoughts and feelings to the painting, to make the painting an object of self-expression. Wang Hsia is credited with inventing the splattered ink style of landscape painting. As described in a previous chapter, this was created from the random configurations of ink that Wang had smeared and daubed while in a drunken state. His innovative approach to painting was important to later generations as a symbol of creative freedom.

It is evident from the descriptions of these and other painters

96 Chou Fang, T'ang dynasty:
Palace Women Adorned with Flowers (details).

active in the second half of the eighth century, that radical changes took place in painting following the High T'ang period. There was a new awareness of the potential of brush and ink, an increased consciousness of the painter's freedom to create and recognition of the painting's potential to contain poetic ideas. Moreover, from the Mid T'ang (766-840), painters gradually gained autonomy, as governmental and social restrictions slackened and a kind of "art for art's sake" movement took hold. All these factors helped to expand the boundaries of painting. Representative of painters who specialized in figure painting and religious subjects at this time was Chou Fang. Pien Lüan earned a reputation for being the finest painter of animals, birds and flowers.

Chou Fang (active ca. 766-804) is best known for his depictions of palace women whom he painted with elegantly proportioned bodies and ample flesh. Clothed in gorgeous silks, Chou Fang's women well represented the aesthetic ideal of the T'ang aristocracy (fig. 96). Chou Fang also added an element of feminine charm to his rendition of the Buddhist divinity Kuan-yin (Avalokitesvara), who was thus transformed from an image of divine, otherworldly solemnity to one of maternal compassion. At the very beginning of the T'ang dynasty, flowers, birds, animals and similar subjects were not especially popular in painting. However, this began to change after the minister Hsüeh Chi earned fame for his paintings of cranes in the Early T'ang. After him, specialists of flowers, feather and fur subjects began to appear. During the reign of Emperor Hsüan-tsung (r. 712-56), a number of painters earned particular acclaim for their painting of horses, including Ts'ao Pa, his disciple Han Kan (ca. 720-80), the father and son Wei Chien and Wei Yen, and Ch'en Hung. Pien Lüan was a court painter during the reign of Emperor Te-tsung. During the Chen-yüan reign (785-804), a gorgeous dancing peacock was presented to the throne as tribute from a western kingdom. Te-tsung ordered Pien Lüan to paint its image in the Hsüan-wu Palace and Pien responded with a painting that captured the myriad transformations of the peacock's plumage. Pien Lüan's paintings of birds, flowers and insects revealed a particular talent for showcasing the splendor of colors. He can be credited with raising the pure aesthetic appreciation of beauty in Chinese painting.

Chapter Three
The Five Dynasties Period and the Sung Dynasty
906~1279

During the Five Dynasties Period, there were two important centers for Chinese painting: the kingdom of Western Shu in modern-day Ssuchuan Province, and the Southern T'ang kingdom located in Chiang-nan, the region south of the Yangtze River. Following the reunification of China under the Sung dynasty, the painters of Shu and Southern T'ang largely congregated at the court in the new capital at Pien-ching (K'ai-feng, Honan). In this manner, not only was there a continuation of artistic activity through the change of dynasties, but there was active promotion by the ruling house. Consequently, painting of the Five Dynasties Period and early Sung can be considered a continuation of trends and developments from the T'ang.

The examples presented in the previous chapter on the early history of painting, from its beginnings to the Tsin dynasty, are almost exclusively limited to figure painting, which indicates its dominance over this long period of time. While images of humans in Han dynasty art well attest to the impressive gains of figure painting, what exists of landscape in this period is limited to the occasional motifs of trees, rocks and hills which serve as a backdrop for figures. During the Wei-Tsin and Six Dynasties Period, images of landscape were painted by Ku K'ai-chih, Wei Hsieh, Tsung Ping, Wang Wei, Chang Seng-yu and others, but there is practically nothing from this period visible today. Moreover, landscapes of this period were given a rather unsympathetic critique by the T'ang dynasty art historian Chang Yen-yüan. There was little logic to the scale and placements of boats, figures and mountains. Mountains and rocks were schematically arranged, like the teeth of a comb or the fingers of one's hand. The overall effect struck Chang Yen-yüan as child-like. Even less successful were attempts to suggest depth and space. Landscape imagery begins to flourish in the Sui dynasty, but always as accompaniment to palaces, pavilions and figures. As narrated in the last chapter, it was not until the T'ang dynasty and the emergence of Li Ssu-hsün, Wu Tao-tzu and Wang Wei that landscape painting began to find its true footing. Li Ssu-hsün used a fine-brush technique to carefully outline the contours of his mountains. The interiors were then filled with mineral blue and green pigments and gold to create a sumptuous image of landscape. He and his blue-and-green landscapes were later regarded as the fountainhead of the Northern School of landscape painting. Wu Tao-tzu was primarily known as a figure painter, but his landscapes, painted with a fast-moving brush, presented an important alternative to the carefully crafted fine-brush style. Wang Wei's landscapes utilized the subtleties of inkwash. His influence in the end was the greatest. Later critics set him in opposition to Li Ssu-hsün as the founder of the Southern School of landscape painting.

By the end of the T'ang dynasty, landscape painting had already reached a stage of high accomplishment, and the art form develops rapidly through the Five Dynasties Period, Northern Sung and Southern Sung. The artists' understanding of nature's elements, their techniques and their theoretical understanding of the art all quickly reach an unprecedented level of maturity. This period witnesses radical changes in composition. From the vertical dominance of the central mountain of Five Dynasties Period and Northern Sung monumental landscape, the artists begin to explore the subtleties of one-corner compositions in the Southern Sung. The vertical axis loses its place of importance to the four corners and the depiction of space gradually emerges as one of the painter's primary concerns. Kuo Hsi speaks of "three distances" in his text on landscape painting, which reveals that by the third quarter of the eleventh century, there already existed a concrete understanding of how space could be suggested in painting. Certainly, this represents a big step from Tsung Ping and his *Preface on Landscape Painting* of six centuries earlier. Various methods for texturing rocks and mountains also emerge during this period, such as Tung Yüan's and Chü-jan's hemp-fiber strokes, Fan K'uan's rain-dot stroke, Kuo Hsi's roiling clouds stroke, Mi Fu's Mi family dot and Li T'ang's ax-cut stroke. These would eventually form the basis for the painter's approach to constructing landscape and constitute one of the most characteristic aspects of Chinese painting. The great masters of landscape painting during this period would have a tremendous influence on the later development of this magnificent art form. They would establish the standards by which all others would be judged.

98 Ching Hao, Five dynasties period: Mount Lu.

97 Li Ch'eng, Five dynasties period:
Luxuriant Forest among Distant Peaks.

Preavious pages
99 Detail, **97**

1. The Northern Tradition of Landscape Painting

We begin with painters active in the northern regions of China, including the provinces of Shansi and Shensi, for whom the mountains in this area served as the inspiration for their paintings. The two representative painters of the early phase of the monumental landscape painting tradition were Ching Hao (fig. 98) and Kuan T'ung (fig. 63), who lived in the tenth century. Ching Hao resided as a hermit in Hung Valley of the T'ai-hang Mountains of Shensi for many years. He claims in a short text on landscape painting to have combined the brushwork of Wu Tao-tzu with the ink-methods of Hsiang Jung and thus to have surpassed them both. Kuan T'ung learned directly from Ching Hao. He is said to have painted the abrupt, tall mountains of Kuan-shan or the Wei River Valley of Shensi. It is difficult to say whether or not genuine paintings by these two masters exist today, but judging from credible attributions and textual descriptions, Ching Hao and Kuan T'ung largely utilized inkwash and depicted towering mountain peaks with strong brushwork comprised of short, staccato strokes. Fan K'uan, who was active about fifty years after Kuan T'ung, can be considered the most prominent master of the painters of this region. The National Palace Museum's "Travelers among Mountains and Streams" (figs. 6, 67, 82) well exemplifies the characteristics of the northern tradition, including an abrubtly rising central massif, whose towering presence overwhelms the viewer, and a forceful technique. Fan K'uan's rain-dot texture strokes build up the eroded, sedimentary rock formations of the high plains of the Yellow River. The slightly rounded mountain peak is constructed of a conglomeration of 'Y'-shaped motifs. This becomes one of the hallmarks of the Fan K'uan style as it was emulated by later painters.

Another important northern area for the development of landscape painting was the Huang-huai Plateau of Shantung Province along the lower reaches of the Yellow River. This region witnessed the emergence of the great landscape master Li Ch'eng (916-67), who combined the wild scenery of the remote plains with a misty atmosphere to create landscapes that were at once desolate and pure. Li Ch'eng's remarkably subtle use of ink allowed his landscapes to appear deep and distant. His paintings often showcased a particular type of tree with branches turned and twisted like crab claws. Set in the bitter cold of a winter scene, these epitomized endurance and ancientness. "Luxuriant Forests and Distant Peaks" (figs. 97, 99), a painting attributed to the master, well exhibits the deep mysterious atmosphere for which Li Ch'eng was famous.

The painter, who synthesized the western and eastern schools of the northern landscape style to establish a truly idealized landscape was Kuo Hsi (ca. 1020-90). He modeled himself after Li Ch'eng, but also received influence from Fan K'uan's style. Kuo Hsi was also a noted painting theorist. His *Lofty Aspirations among Forests and Streams* counts as one of the single most important texts on landscape painting, explicating both the essentials and the details of the art. The magnificence of nature is presented in his painting "Early Spring" (figs. 10, 13) with an animated air that befits the painting's theme. The "roiling clouds" mode of texturing and "crab-claw trees," which Kuo Hsi adopted from Li Ch'eng, are two of the enduring motifs associated with Kuo Hsi's style through the later dynasties.

2. The Southern Tradition of Landscape Painting

Representative of the southern landscape painting tradition are the Five Dynasties Period artists Tung Yüan and the monk Chü-jan, both of whom

Left
101 Chü-jan, Five dynasties period:
Layered Mountains and Dense Woods.

Below above
100 Tung Yüan, Five dynasties period:
Wintry Grove, Layered Banks.

were active in the Southern T'ang Kingdom. Tung Yüan painted the "true mountains" of the Chiang-nan region (fig. 100). His brushwork differs distinctly from the works of Ching Hao and Kuan T'ung, whose forceful approaches are eschewed for a more placid style. Tung Yüan does not carefully chisel out lofty peaks of extraordinary appearance, but rather strings together dots and dashes in a kind of pointillist technique so that the scenery of his paintings only comes into focus when one steps back from them. Chü-jan is said to have studied with Tung Yüan. His paintings largely employ hemp-fiber texture strokes which effectively describe the earthy hills of the Yangtze River region (fig. 101). Small round rock formations, sometimes referred to as "alum-head," are often seen on Chü jan's mountain peaks and within the forested slopes of his hills. The pure, unaffected brush and inkwork that infuses his landscapes with a profound atmosphere earned the label *t'ien-chen* "natural" from later critics.

In the first half of the Northern Sung, the landscapes of Li Ch'eng and Fan K'uan rode a crest of popularity. Tung Yüan and Chü-jan, in contrast, received little attention. This situation changed in the late years of the Northern Sung, when the highly influential critic Mi Fu (1052-1107) strongly promoted Tung Yüan's painting. Mi Fu and his son Mi Yu-jen (1074-1151) were also important landscape painters. The so-called Mi family landscape, descriptive of the misty atmosphere of Chiang-nan, is well represented by Mi Yu-jen's "Cloudy Mountains" of 1130 (fig. 102). Rounded mountains are wrapped in tumbling clouds and mist in a display of animated transformation. Mi Yu-jen's paintings commonly reveal myriad subtleties of ink, an aspect of painting which in the end became one of the defining features of the Chinese painting tradition. Contemporary to Mi Yu-jen was Chiang Shen (ca. 1090-1138), who also was a painter of the southern landscape of Chiang-nan in the tradition of Tung Yüan and Chü-jan. Chiang Shen's landscapes anticipate the developments of the Yüan dynasty.

102 Mi Yu-jen, Sung dynasty: Cloudy Mountains (detail).

103 Yen Wen-kuei, Sung dynasty: Towers and Pavilions among Mountains and Rivers (detail).

Of course, the great masters of landscape during the Northern Sung are not limited to these few painters. Yen Wen-kuei, for example, painted landscapes of stern, dramatic character (fig. 103) and Hsü Tao-ning (ca. 1000-after 1052) was known for landscapes of imposing, heroic manner (figs. 14, 15). Both painters were of the first rank.

The division here between painters of the northern and southern landscapes is not to be confused with the theory of the Northern and Southern Schools that was promoted by Tung Ch'i-ch'ang in the late phase of the Ming dynasty. In the Five Dynasties Period and Northern Sung, the landscapes that were lodged in the artists' breasts were inseparable from the real landscapes they had traversed during their lifetimes. Even in the Yüan dynasty, paintings still revealed a strong link to the exterior world. Kuo Hsi wrote:

> In recent times, painters of Wu and Yüeh (the Chiang-nan region) sketch the refined hills of the southeast and those of Hsien-Ch'in (central Shensi Province) paint the broad, stalwart manner of the landscape of Kuan-lung.

Kuo Hsi thus provides a contemporary's confirmation of the integral relationship between the actual and painted landscapes of the time and the appropriate division of northern and southern regional styles. Tung Ch'i-ch'ang also spoke directly of this matter.

> Li Ssu-hsün painted the mountains beyond the sea, Tung Yüan those of Chiang-nan, Mi Yu-jen those of Nan-hsü (Chen-chiang, Kiangsu Province), Li T'ang those of Chung-chou (Honan Province), Ma Yüan those of Ch'ien-t'ang (Hangchou, Chekiang Province), Chao Meng-fu those of T'iao-cha (northern Chekiang) and Huang Kung-wang those of Hai-yü (east of Ch'ang-shu, Kiangsu).

Extant paintings from the Northern Sung through Yüan largely substantiate Tung Ch'i-ch'ang's observation. The limited one-corner compositions of Southern Sung date well suit the waterscapes of the regions around the Huai and Yangtze Rivers. Similarly, the wet marshlands and riverine landscape portrayed in Yüan paintings are elegant testimony to the congregation of painters in the Chiang-nan region from Hangchou to Wu-hsing to Suchou during this time.

In summary, the special characteristic of Northern Sung landscape painting is not simply its refinement or breadth, but rather its sense of tangible substance. Whether it is the imposing majesty of a central mountain or the weight and texture of forested hills, rocks and streams, all reveal the intrinsic, concentrated power of nature.

3. The Bird-and-Flower Styles of Hsü Hsi and Huang Ch'üan

The regional differences noted in landscape painting of the Five Dynasties Period and Northern Sung to a certain degree also pertain to bird-and-flower painting. Specifically, two schools emerge: the school of Hsü Hsi who was active in the Southern T'ang, and that of Huang Ch'üan who was active in the kingdom of Western Shu.

The Western Shu kingdom, geographically removed from the T'ang capital of Ch'ang-an and the numerous conflicts and violence that afflicted the central plains towards the end of the T'ang dynasty, was a place of refuge for many scholars and artists. The celebrated bird-and-flower painter Tiao Kuang-yin, for example, carried with him to Ssuchuan the refined and beautiful style of bird-and-flower painting that had developed around the T'ang court. Huang Ch'üan (903-68), Tiao's student, was employed at the court of the Western Shu (fig. 104). After the Western Shu fell to the conquering Sung, he remained a court painter, though now at Pien-ching for the new Sung dynasty. Throughout his lifetime as a master of bird-and-flower painting, Huang Ch'üan was engaged in the depiction of the rare species collected for the enjoyment of the royal family. These beautiful subjects were matched with a resplendent, colorful manner of depiction that was full of detail. This style of painting was continued by Huang Ch'üan's two sons,

104 Huang Ch'üan, Five dynasties period: Sketches from Life (detail).

Huang Chü-ts'ai (933- after 993) and Huang Pao-ts'ai, and the following generation as well.

The Southern T'ang inherited the rich cultural traditions that had developed in the Chiang-nan area since the Eastern Tsin. The representative bird-and-flower painter here was Hsü Hsi, an official whose extensive travels exposed him to a wide range of flora and fauna. Hsü Hsi painted the trees, flowers, fruits, birds and insects that he saw in the wilds of the river country. His style of painting was less meticulous, with more reliance on brush and inkwork than color, so in both subject matter and style, Hsü Hsi's art contrasted sharply with the work of Huang Ch'üan. In the Sung dynasty, the contrast was phrased, "The luxury of Huang, the untamed quality of Hsü."

Although Hsü Hsi is primarily known for painting that explored the freedom of brush and ink, he is also known to have painted in a richly colorful style—the kind of palace-style flower painting that was well-suited for decorating the walls of aristocratic residences (see p.64 and fig. 42). In such paintings, flowers and rocks are built up to create a rich tapestry-like design against a mineral-blue background. Huang Ch'üan also was not limited by the style for which he is best-known: in addition to his polychromatic paintings, he is said to have painted bamboo in ink alone. Nonetheless, the application of color remained one of the dominant features of painting at this time and in this regard, Hsü Hsi and his style of ink painting represented a new direction (fig. 105).

105 Anonymous, Sung dynasty: Bamboo in Snow.

4. The Golden Age of Palace Art

The humanistic arts flourished under the active promotion of the Sung court. Early in the dynasty, a Painter Service was established in the Artisans Institute of the Palace Domestic Service. There had, in fact, been a long history in China of institutionalized services specifically created to provide arts and crafts to the court. Painters assisted the emperor in disseminating moral and governmental teachings by painting didactic subjects, and for the daily needs of the extensive royal family, specialized craftsmen were employed to make beautiful, refined utensils. To meet both private and public demands, it was only natural for institutions to be set up by the court and among these was the Imperial Painting Academy.

There are records of professional painters already being employed by the court during the Spring and Autumn and Warring States Periods of the Chou dynasty. Specialized services were established at the Yellow (imperial) Gates during the Han dynasty and there are records of related institutions in existence during the Six Dynasties Period. In general, the Imperial Painting Academy of the Sung dynasty developed out of trends established during the late T'ang and was carried forward in the Five Dynasties Period by the kingdoms of Southern T'ang and Western Shu. Under Sung T'ai-tsu's rule, painters employed by the courts of these two kingdoms entered his own dynasty's Painter Service of the Artisans own as the Imperial Painting Academy. Nurtured by the court with material support and institutionalized training, these professional painters throughout the Sung dynasty attained a level of accomplishment that far outdistanced anything achieved before or since.

Bird-and-flower painting of the Imperial Painting Academy during the Northern Sung was, from the beginning, dominated by the influence of Huang Ch'üan and Huang Chü-ts'ai who had been transplanted from Western Shu. Their popularity can be ascribed to the court's natural attraction to a refined, colorful aesthetic which matched the luxurious environment enjoyed by the aristocracy. "The luxury of Huang," as it was called, set the standard early in the Sung. By the reign of Emperor Shen-tsung (1068-85), however, a new, livelier style of painting was created by artists such as Ts'ui Po and Wu Yüan-yu. This transformation of style can be illustrated by comparing Huang Chü-ts'ai's "Mountain Magpie, Sparrows and Bramble" (fig. 106) with Ts'ui Po's "Magpies and Hare" (fig. 107). The focus of Huang Chü-ts'ai's composition is set squarely on the centrally placed mountain magpie. The scene is exceedingly stable, and the atmosphere is both weighty and antique—characteristics of early Northern Sung painting in general. In contrast, the focus of Ts'ui Po's "Magpies and Hare" is on the strong diagonal pull between the upper right and lower left portions of the composition, which draws the viewer deeply into the drama of the painting. As for their techniques, Huang Chü-ts'ai uses understated, restrained brushwork throughout his work while "Magpies and Hare" demonstrates ceaseless variation. In addition to the flying, horizontal brush-traces which are used in the foreground slope and are immediately noticed, the lines that describe the branches and bamboo exhibit a wide range of modulation and speed. Perhaps the trends revealed by Ts'ui Po's "unrestrained style" are related to Hsü Hsi's manner of painting, which for many years had not been regarded seriously.

One can hardly speak of the Imperial Painting Academy without mentioning the artistically inclined emperor who presided over the last years of the Northern Sung: Chao Chi, otherwise known as Hui-tsung (r. 1100-25). Early in the Sung dynasty, the court had followed the earlier systems of organization employed for the Hanlin Academy during the Five Dynasties Period for recruiting and establishing artisans. With Hui-tsung's rule, however, important changes were made in the recruitment of painters and their training at the painting academy. During the Cheng-ho reign period (1111-17), professional painters for the first time were tested according to

The Six Classified Categories of Painters in the Hanlin Academy

1. Painter-in-attenddence (tai-chao)
2. Usher (chih-hou)
3. Student of the arts (i-hsueh)
4. Painting school director (hua-hsüen cheng)
5. Student (hsüeh-sheng)
6. Servitor (kung-feng).

106 Huang Chü-ts'ai, Sung dynasty: Mountain Magpie, Sparrows and Bramble.

107 Ts'ui Po, Sung dynasty: Magpies and Hare.

criteria established by the National University. As described in an earlier chapter (see p.24), lines from ancient poems were used as painting themes. The Imperial Painting Academy's adoption of themes to test the creative abilities of the artists and the introduction of a humanistic curriculum raised the aesthetic consciousness of the painters and allowed painting to become an art of pure, spiritual enjoyment.

Hui-tsung's own abilities as a calligrapher and painter were of the first rank and from his extant works (fig. 78), one can understand his interest in nurturing and developing the various talents at the Imperial Painting Academy. Hui-tsung had paintings from the imperial collection made available for the painters' study. The painters were taught to paint Buddhist and Taoist subjects, figures, landscapes, birds, beasts, flowers, bamboo and architectural subjects. In addition, they were trained in lexical works such as the *Shuo-wen chieh-tzu*, *Erh-ya* and other books related to the Confucian classics. The painters were rewarded well for their work and their positions carried a measure of status. They were allowed to wear the fish pendant (a symbol of status) and when presented to the emperor, they were set just behind members of the Calligraphy School. From system of summoning and testing, the Imperial Painting Academy managed to bring all capable artisans to the court, where they were encouraged and strictly trained in the service to the emperor. Hui-tsung was not the only one to patronize the arts in this fashion. During the Southern Sung as well, the Imperial Painting Academy was reestablished, producing representative painters of the period such as Li T'ang, Liu Sung-nien, Ma Yüan and Hsia Kuei. An academic style was thus established—one of the defining schools of painting in the history of Chinese art.

108 Li Kung-lin, Sung dynasty: The Five Horses (detail).

5. The Birth of Literati Painting

In any profession, success demands immersion in training and dedication to one's work. It is no different with painting, which is commonly recognized as a professional skill—a metier for specialists. Yet, in the Chinese painting tradition, it is not uncommon to find celebrated painters who were other things first: emperors, high officials and men of letters. Moreover, their accomplishments outside of art were often considerable. How did it come to pass that these important figures became painters as well? In Chinese society, education always emphasized elevating one's personal character and virtue. Painting and calligraphy offered relief from social demands. Literati painting, as the artistic products of these scholars has come to be known, represents one of the defining features of the Chinese painting tradition.

There are some early examples of literary figures who became prominent painters. The most notable was Wang Wei (701-61) who once said, "In this life I have mistakenly become a man of letters; in a former life I must have been a painting master." Wang Wei's fame was such that he was later considered to be the patriarch of literati painting. In spirit, literati painting is an art of personal expression: one paints without restraint, frankly and directly conveying one's feelings and sense of self on the painting surface. Yet, it emerges during a period in Chinese painting history when verisimilitude is realized with the greatest of results. Just as Sung painting presents a degree of realism never before matched, the famous scholar and official Su Shih (1036-1101) utters his famous objection: "Those who discuss painting in terms of lifelikeness have the understanding of a child." Su Shih's point is that quality in painting is not to be measured solely on the basis of whether or not the painted image looks like its subject. More important is its spirit. Su Shih and his circle, which included Huang T'ing-chien (1045-1105), Li Kung-lin (ca. 1049-1106), Mi Fu (1052-1107), Wen T'ung (1019-79) (fig. 110) and others, were all leading literary figures of the time. The revolutionary spirit that they brought to painting may not have been all that influential in their own era, but it provided the groundwork for the fundamental changes that took place in the Yüan dynasty two hundred years later.

Su Shih himself was adept at painting bamboo. One time while supervising in the Examination Office, he was inspired to paint but found himself without ink; all that was available was the red cinnabar used for correcting student exams. Su Shih used this to paint red bamboo, which he later showed to his friends. "Where in the world does bamboo grow red?" his friends asked, but Su Shih had a ready response: "And where does it grow with the colors of black ink?"

Su Shih's friend and contemporary, Li Kung-lin, opened a new phase in figure painting in the late Northern Sung. Figure painting at the beginning of the Northern Sung faithfully continued the styles inherited from the Five Dynasties Period. The Wu Tao-tzu style, in particular, provided the standard for mural painting of Buddhist and Taoist subjects, as exemplified by "Procession of Taoist Immortals to Pay Homage to the King of Heaven" (fig. 109) which is a work attributed to Wu Tsung-yüan (d. 1050), one of the most famous painters working in the Wu Tao-tzu style at this time. Li Kung-lin also studied the Wu Tao-tzu style early in his career, but his researches also included the style of Ku K'ai-chih. Li was an educated man and as an expression of his scholarly approach to painting, he liked to limit his paintings to modulated brush-lines alone. This kind of painting, in which

109 Wu Tsung-yüan, Sung dynasty: Procession of Taoist Immortals to Pay Homage to the King of Heaven (detail).

color was not applied, was later given the label *pai-miao* or "plain drawing." In fact, Wu Tao-tzu, in a sense, began *pai-miao* painting by concentrating almost entirely on the line drawing of the murals. Light colors were later added to create what was then called the "Wu fashion." Li Kung-lin's *pai-miao* goes a step further, reducing the painting to pure monochrome and thus displaying an antique and refined air which contrasted with the bold, elemental energy of Wu Tao-tzu's painting. Li Kung-lin also excelled at horse painting. "Five Horses" (fig. 108) is a representative example of his painting in this genre.

110 Wen T'ung, Sung dynasty: Ink Bamboo.

6. Painting of the Southern Sung—the Magic of Space

A major transformation in painting began to take place after the flight of the Sung court south, which marked the beginning of the Southern Sung Period in 1127. With the court's migration across the Yangtze River to Hangchou, the economic and cultural center of China also moved to the Chiang-nan region. The southern landscape provided painters with new subject matter and new inspiration. One highly influential painter during the transitional period was Li T'ang (active ca. 1100-1150) (fig. 39), who served in Hui-tsung's painting academy during the Hsuan-ho reign before crossing the river south to become a major figure in the academy reestablished by Emperor Kao-tsung during the Shao-hsing period (1131-62). "Whispering Pines in the Gorges" (fig. 33) was painted while Li T'ang was still at the Northern Sung Imperial Painting Academy and it maintains the imposing appearance of the monumental landscape painting tradition. Heaven above, earth below—the utter clarity of nature's order provides the guiding principle, as Li T'ang wields a sharp and powerful brush to chisel out the myriad facets of the hard rock's surface. However, with the move to the south and the gentle atmospheric landscape of the Ch'ien-t'ang River area surrounding Hangchou, a tremendous change occurs. Li T'ang himself said, "Snowy village shrouded in mist, river shoal wrapped in fog—such sights easily enter the eye, but describing them is hard." The captivating scenes of which Li T'ang writes, subtle and suffused with heavy atmosphere, are precisely the subject matter of the Southern Sung artists. Representative are Ma Yüan and Hsia Kuei, active during the reign of Emperor Ning-tsung (r. 1194-1224) in the middle of the Southern Sung. Ma Yüan's "Mountain Stroll in Spring" (fig. 111) and Hsia Kuei's "Gazing at the Waterfall" (fig. 21) limit themselves to the depiction of the corner of a lakeshore or a small portion of a mountain. These kinds of scenes are what led to the labels "One-corner Ma" and "Half-a-side Hsia." These unpainted portions effectively suggest unlimited space, and it provides the means for the viewer's eye and thoughts to be

111 Ma Yüan, Sung dynasty: Mountain Stroll in Spring.

庭院秋戲

壬寅竹坨識

112 Su Han-ch'en, Sung dynasty: Children Playing in the Autumn Garden.   (detail *left*)

114 Ma Ho-chih, Sung dynasty:
Ancient Tree by Flowing Water.

carried far beyond the painted images. From Northern to Southern Sung, the complex is slowly replaced by the simple, the abbreviated and the suggestive. All of the Southern Sung landscape painters adopted the approach represented here by Ma Yüan and Hsia Kuei.

The Southern Sung period witnessed the great flowering of fan and album leaf painting. Refined and exquisite, these small works are immensely attractive and they amply demonstrate the success of the Southern Sung academy which produced generation after generation of talented artists. For figure painting, all manner of themes and subject matter were explored— beautiful women, children, historical narratives, genre scenes, portraits, and religious icons and stories. In the early phase of the Southern Sung, the refined, detailed manner of Northern Sung painting was continued, as exemplified by Su Han-ch'en's "Children Playing in the Autumn Garden" (fig. 112). The look of concentration on the children's faces as they play with the balancing toy is captured with unerring skill. Even a camera would be hard pressed to reproduce with such extraordinary detail the fine black hair that graces their heads. Liu Sung-nien's "Lohan (Arhat)" (fig. 113) is painted with a firm, pliant brush that magnificently conveys the divinity of the Buddhist sage with its subtle twists and turns. Ma Ho-chih's technique is particularly unusual (fig. 114). Movement is engendered within an extremely soft brush-mode that has earned the label "locust stroke." Ma Ho-chih used it to describe figures as well as landscape. For an example of scenes from common life, one need to look no further than Li Sung's "Village Peddler and Playing Children" (fig. 115), a painting which may never be surpassed in refinement and detail.

7. The Abbreviated Brush

Perhaps it is the natural course of things that no sooner when one extreme is reached, then an equally strong movement in the other direction begins. So

113 Liu Sung-nien, Sung dynasty:
Lohan (Arhat).

156

115 Li Sung, Sung dynasty:
Village Peddler with Playing Children.

117 Mu-ch'i, Sung dynasty: Six Persimmons.

it was with the level of refined, meticulous realism that the Southern Sung painters were able to achieve: others came along and produced something entirely different. The artist who best shows the rejection is Liang K'ai, master of the "abbreviated brush" and "splattered ink." Liang K'ai was originally a painter in attendance at the Southern Sung imperial academy who excelled at both landscapes and figures, but his personality was a bit strange. He refused to accept the "golden belt" award that was bequeathed to him by the emperor, "hanging it up within the academy to pursue wine and personal pleasures, thus earning the nickname Madman Liang." His new style of painting was rough and simplified; the brush moved extremely fast and forms were modeled in abbreviated fashion. One of his representative works "Inkwash Painted Immortal" (fig. 51) was introduced in Chapter Five. Another notable painting in this style is "Li Po Chanting a Poem while Strolling" (fig. 116). With a mere handful of strokes, Liang K'ai captures the lofty independence of the famous T'ang poet who seems to have entered a realm all his own. Most beautiful of all are the shifting tones of brushwork that describe Li Po's robe. This style of painting, in fact, did not suddenly appear with Liang K'ai. In Ssuchuan during the Five Dynasties Period, Shih K'o was fond of painting strange figures with a novel style that ignored the standard rules. One painting attributed to him, "The Two Patriarchs Harmonizing Their Minds" (fig. 118), reveals a fast-moving, powerful brush used to describe the sleeping sage's clothing and this anticipates Liang K'ai's style. The only difference is that Liang K'ai's painting is even more simplified.

Slightly later than Liang K'ai was the monk Mu-ch'i. Like Liang K'ai, Mu-ch'i is said to have been fond of drink and his style of painting seems to have come from the same mold. Whereas Liang K'ai excelled at work's forte was in spreading the ink. In his painting "Six Persimmons" (fig. 117), ink alone is used, but with extraordinary range. From the sharp black brushstrokes that describe the fruits' stems to the shifting washes that describe their flesh, Mu-ch'i demonstrates the heights of skill with the simplest of means. Substance is born from utter simplicity and with a flavor that is at once antique and refined. The painting would seem to suggest the profundity of the Ch'an (Zen) teachings to which Mu-ch'i devoted his life as a monk.

Left
116 Liang K'ai, Sung dynasty: Li Po Chanting a Poem while Strolling (detail).

Right
118 Shih K'o, Five dynasties period: The Two Patriarchs Harmonizing Their Minds.

澹煙練色互凑
清明罨畫峰
汀洲有情芳
把鵲白搆靈
難翻翻隨勢巾
兩相爭

右咏鵲山
乾隆戊辰春書
臨筆

Chapter Four

The Yüan Dynasty

1279~1368

1. The Establishment of Literati Painting

With the fall of the Sung dynasty, the Imperial Painting Academy, which had been the primary source for painting through the Southern Sung, also came to an end. The Yüan court did not reinstate the system of officially sponsored painting. Occasionally there were painters who served at the Yüan court, but nominally, at least, in another context. Liu Kuan-tao, for example, who painted "Kublai Khan Hunting" and "Whiling away the Summer" (fig. 120), served as an official in the Imperial Wardrobe Service which was totally unrelated to a painting academy. His painting followed the finely detailed, realistic style of the Northern Sung, with bright colors often applied. This is quite different from what proved to be the main current of painting in the Yüan—that of the literati.

Because the Yüan was a foreign dynasty ruled by the Mongols, a majority of Chinese scholars were either barred from assuming their customary roles as officials or were unwilling to do so. Many turned to painting and calligraphy as an outlet for their energy. This large-scale participation in painting by the literati had the effect of transforming style. The art became a more subjective and personal expression of individual feelings. With this transformation, the two fundamental styles of Chinese painting were established: Sung and Yüan. As described earlier, literati participation in the art of painting had already taken place in the Northern Sung, with figures such as Su Shih and Li Kung-lin both promoting and actively painting. It was not until the Yüan dynasty, however, that literati painting truly began to flower.

The key figure in the transformation was Chao Meng-fu (1254-1322). Another influential person was Chao's fellow townsman, friend and teacher Ch'ien Hsüan (ca. 1235- after 1301). These two are reported to have had a discussion concerning what it was that comprises scholar's painting, *shih-tai-fu hua*. Chao Meng-fu asked Ch'ien Hsüan for a definition of "scholarly spirit" *(shih-ch'i)* in painting. Ch'ien replied:

> It is the clerical (i.e. unadorned) style. By studying the history of painting, one can determine it. Although wingless, it can still fly. If this 'scholarly spirit' is missing, then painting descends to the heterodox path. The more skillful painting may be, the further it drifts (from the proper way). There is another point: it must be something that cares nothing for worldly opinion. It has no concern for praise or censure.

The "scholarly spirit" discussed in this passage refers to a quality unique to the educated elite. It is what differentiates their painting from the work of professional artists. Painstaking refinement of style is rejected, and even less so the favorable opinion of collectors and

Left
119 Chao Meng-fu, Yüan dynasty: Autumn Colors on the Ch'üeh and Hua Mountains (detail).

161

120 Liu Kuan-tao, Yüan dynasty: Whiling away the Summer.

public that would guarantee a ready market. The scholar-artist paints with no thought for accolades or criticism. This concept of painting for oneself alone not only bespeaks individual creativity, we can say that it is the essential element that allows painting to stand as an independent art. It is for this reason that literati painting gained in prominence to be recognized as the most representative form of Chinese painting.

Ch'ien Hsüan and Chao Meng-fu worked hard to wash away the coarse, undisciplined styles that were current in the late phase of the Southern Sung and to resurrect the styles of the T'ang and Northern Sung. Chao Meng-fu, in particular, was the leader in this movement. This was a person blessed with extraordinary natural talent, a calligrapher and painter worthy of the label great master. Chao promoted the concept of prizing "antique ideas." He predominantly followed the styles of Tung Yüan and Chü-jan in his landscape painting, emphasizing in particular the expressive qualities of brush and ink. Chao Meng-fu also upraised the theory that painting and calligraphy shared the same origins. It was he who pronounced and demonstrated how the methods of writing characters could be employed in painting. Chao Meng-fu's "Autumn Colors on the Ch'üeh and Hua Mountains" (figs. 119, 121), a light and elegant example of the blue-green landscape genre, exhibits an unadorned, lucid linear beauty in a calm and peaceful scene. Later critics regarded this style of painting as "possessing the fineness of T'ang without the delicacy, having the forthrightness of Sung while eliminating its breadth." Such painting adopts the approach of "returning to the ancients" (fu-ku),

121 Chao Meng-fu, Yüan dynasty: Autumn Colors on the Ch'üeh and Hua Mountains.

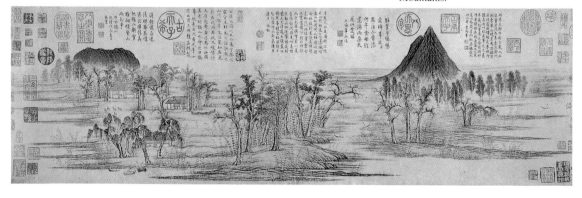

but not through careful imitation of earlier styles. Rather, Chao Meng-fu seeks to merge with the spirit of earlier painters. He seeks spiritual likeness, as opposed to formal likeness, and in so doing, opens the path for Yüan painting to move away from the restraints that tie a painting to its subject's appearance and allow it to pursue the beauties of brush and ink.

Representative landscape painters of the early Yüan include Sheng Mou, Chu Te-jun (1294-1365) and T'ang Ti (ca. 1286-1354), all of whom were influenced by Chao Meng-fu. More distantly, they adopted the styles of the earlier monumental landscape painters Li Ch'eng and Kuo Hsi. At the same time, the styles of Tung Yüan and Chü-jan, as well as the ink-plays of Mi Fu and Mi Yu-jen, were also highly regarded in the early Yüan. One major painter who continued this style of painting cloudy mountain landscapes, molding it in his own individual manner, was Chao Meng-fu's contemporary Kao K'o-kung (1248-1310). Chao Meng-fu's student Sheng Mou (active ca. 1310-60) utilized neat, orderly brushwork to paint the river scenery of Chiang-nan. Although the outward appearance of his paintings recalls the Li Ch'eng-Kuo Hsi school of landscape, intrinsically more is owed directly to Chao Meng-fu.

The aim of literati painting is personal amusement and relaxation, but there is room in this recreation for the expression of one's ideals and feelings. Paintings that may appear to have been quickly done, with little if any thought, can in fact contain the direct expression of individual sentiment. Personal experiences find expression through art—as Su Shih said of the bamboo painter Wen T'ung (fig. 110), "What is not exhausted through his poetry overflows to become calligraphy and transforms to become painting." Bamboo becomes a popular subject for painting in the Yüan dynasty as well, for this "gentleman" of the natural world served as a personal symbol for the scholar: "One stem, casual and easy, possesses my true feelings; several branches, deep blue-green, dispel vulgar thoughts." In literati painting, simplicity and transcendence are valued. Colors are used sparingly while ink and inkwash are given greater prominence. That pure, deep calm that characterizes ink painting establishes one important facet of literati painting. A literati painting must be painted well, but beyond that one seeks the quality of the person behind the brush. This evaluation of painting beyond the painting is something unique to the Chinese tradition.

2. The Four Great Masters of the Yüan

The representative landscape painters of the Yüan dynasty are Huang Kung-wang, Wu Chen, Ni Tsan and Wang Meng—the Four Great Masters of the Yüan. All four were lofty minded scholars who, living under the control of a foreign regime, rejected personal fame and fortune. Some chose to live as Taoists, others as gentlemen-recluses on family property, but each exhibited a proud, independent spirit and each one channeled personal emotions and frustrations to poetry, calligraphy and painting. They came from various directions in art and their individual styles differed, but each was able to develop certain merits of the tradition they inherited.

Huang Kung-wang (1269-1354) reveals in his masterpiece "Dwelling in the Fu-ch'un Mountains" (figs. 17, 122) elements of the Northern Sung tradition as he describes the scenery along the Fu-ch'un River of Chekiang Province. This, however, is certainly not a reincarnation of Northern Sung landscape painting. The artist used a concise system of brush strokes, and the result is a style that is elegant, lucid and light. This scroll, which significantly influenced the later tradition of landscape painting, exemplifies the style of inkwash landscape to which later literati painters would aspire.

Wu Chen (1280-1354) inherited the mantle of the tenth century painter Chü-jan. His extant works demonstrate a particular fondness for the fisherman theme (fig. 123). For rocks and mountain slopes, Wu Chen employed a flat, direct brush-stroke which imparts a feeling of age and plainness to his landscapes. He also excelled at painting ink bamboo, continuing the tradition of the Sung painter Wen T'ung, but with a touch of untrammeled buoyancy.

Left
122 Huang Kung-wang, Yüan dynasty: Dwelling in the Fu-ch'un Mountains (detail).

Right
123 Wu Chen, Yüan dynasty: Hermit Fisherman on Lake Tung-t'ing.

Ni Tsan (1301-74) provides the paramount example of the simplified style of landscape painting. Typically, his river landscapes consist of a small slope with a few trees or shrubs and a simple pavilion at the bottom of his compositions and then a line or two of distant mountains (figs. 11, 124). Ni Tsan's transparent and airy brushwork infuses his landscapes with a sense of remote purity and it is because of this sense of removal that later critics consider the artist the most representative of the "untrammeled" class. Ni Tsan directly stated that he "paints only to express the untrammeled spirit in his breast." This statement later became one of the important foundations for the literati tradition of painting.

124 Ni Tsan, Yüan dynasty: The Jung-hsi Studio (detail).

Wang Meng (1308-85), a grandson of Chao Meng-fu, reveals an eclectic blending of the styles of Ching Hao, Kuan T'ung, Tung Yüan and Chü-jan. With their overflowing abundance of detail, his paintings present a precisely antithetical image to that of Ni Tsan. In this "Lin-wu Grotto at Chü-ch'ü" (fig. 125), the composition is completely filled with the strange rock formations of the grotto, a few scattered trees, rippling waves and strikingly strong colors. This is a novel style of painting—something unseen in the earlier tradition.

125 Wang Meng, Yüan dynasty: Lin-wu Grotto at Chü-ch'ü.

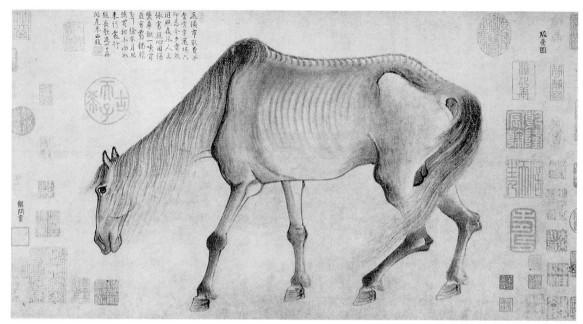

126 Kung K'ai, Yüan dynasty: Emaciated Horse.

3. The Simple and Untrammeled Style of Bird-and-Flower and Figure Painting

The influence of literati painting also reached to the genres of bamboo, birds-and-flowers and animals. Again, colors were largely replaced by ink and inkwash. Subjects high in symbolic content were often chosen to represent the scholar ideal, such as pines, bamboo and blossoming plum. Chao Meng-fu's older relative, Chao Meng-chien (1199-1256), helped begin this trend, painting the theme of the "three friends of winter" (pine, bamboo and plum) in one composition. Under the foreign rule of the Mongols, this manner of lodging one's thoughts, ideals and personality in symbolic subjects became a trend. One example is Kung K'ai's (1222-1307) painting of an emaciated horse (fig. 126), which, according to the artist's own poetic inscription above, "casts a shadow like a mountain on the sandy bank in the setting sun." The heroic steed represents an unbowed gentleman, suffering under the oppression of overlords with whom he refuses to cooperate. Another example is the "rootless" orchid painted by Cheng Ssu-hsiao (1241-1318) (fig. 127), which declares that the ground had been taken away by foreign people.

The most common subject in this type of painting was ink bamboo. In fact, ink bamboo becomes so popular at this time that one could call it the most representative type of Yüan dynasty painting. Chao Meng-fu was the leader in this trend, promoting the notion of the convertibility of calligraphy and painting. Among the other prominent bamboo painters of the Yüan, Li K'an (1245-1320) must be counted as the most important. Li K'an's bamboo painting continued the "sketching-from-nature" style established by Wen T'ung. In addition, Li K'an authored treatises on bamboo painting, in which he describes the characteristics of different types of bamboo as well as painting techniques. "Emerging from the Wall" (fig. 130), a small fan painting by Li K'an, presents a handsome sprig of bamboo as we

128 Wang Yüan, Yüan dynasty: Birds, Bamboo and Rock.

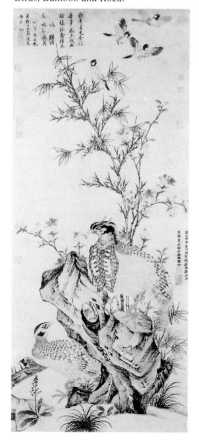

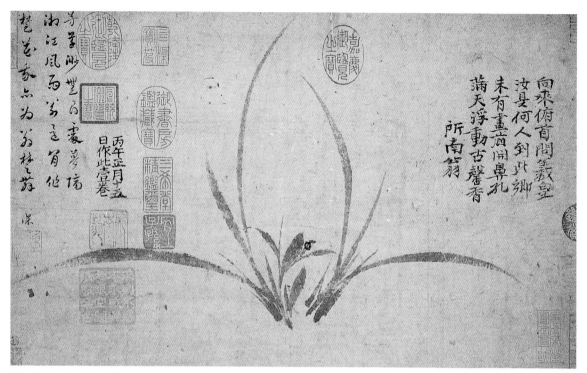

向來俯首問羲皇
汝是何人到此鄉
未有畫前開鼻孔
滿天浮動古馨香
所南翁

楚芒茫兮遠莫歸

湘江風雨泣幽衣

玉筆沙兮世界夢诗

丙午正月五
日作此壹卷

127 Cheng Ssu-hsiao, Yüan dynasty: Orchid.

129 Yen Hui, Yüan dynasty: Drunken Immortal (detail).

might see casually lifting our heads to look through a window. Wu Chen was a superb painter of bamboo in addition to landscape. Others well-known for bamboo painting were K'o Chiu-ssu (1290-1343) and Ku An (ca. 1295-1370).

The great master of bird-and-flower painting in the Yüan dynasty was Wang Yüan (1310-66), who, early in his career, received the teaching of Chao Meng-fu. He also studied the bird-and-flower painting of the Sung academy, but his paintings, exemplified by "Birds, Bamboo and Rock" (fig. 128), exhibit a touch of the coarseness and emphasis of ink that characterizes the emerging literati tradition. Chang Chung, active in the middle of the Yüan, applied light colors for a soft, elegant style. At the end of the Yüan, Wang Mien (1287-1359) specialized in plum blossom painting. Each of these artists painted classic examples of literati-style bird-and-flower painting.

Figure painting in the Yüan dynasty provided grounds for the reemergence and flourishing of the *pai-miao* "plain drawing" technique. Chao Meng-fu, again, provided leadership. In contrast to Sung dynasty figure painting, whether it is in the bold, simplified style, or finely detailed *kung-pi* style, Yüan painters tend to seek the quiet beauty of brush-and-ink that characterizes the literati aesthetic. One painter worth introducing is Yen Hui, whose paintings have long been praised for being rich in movement and liveliness. A detail from Yen Hui's "Drunken Immortal" (fig. 129) corroborates this critique.

Sung dynasty painters painted what they saw. They emphasized nature and learned by sketching from life. Yüan painters relied more on intuitive understanding. The heart takes the place of the eye, as the inclination now was to "sketch ideas" *(hsieh-i)*. These two currents set the pattern for painting through the Ming and Ch'ing dynasties.

4. Differences and Similarities between Sung and Yüan Painting

There is no genre more important in Chinese painting than landscape, which had already enjoyed a long history of development before attaining a level of maturity in the West. Reviewing some of the works of the great masters that have already been introduced, we can analyze landscape painting's stylistic development between the Sung and Yüan dynasties and offer a few observations.

The central line of focus of landscape painting of the Five Dynasties Period and Northern Sung is towards the front face of the main mountain. This orientation emphasizes the height and majesty of the mountain's scene. Fan K'uan's "Travelers among Mountains and Streams" is the classic example: face to face, one is confronted with an awesome display of nature's power. There is a profound observation of the surrounding world that underlies such painting. The artist edits images to create a landscape, but the painting remains so remarkably objective in appearance that the viewer can sit, wander, repose and travel in this re-created world.

In both their choice of scenery and their approach to rendering it in painting, artists of the Southern Sung were remarkably different from their Northern Sung counterparts. The focal point shifts from a main, central mountain to a single hill and valley; from a broad, overwhelming scene suggestive of nature in its totality to a small, removed corner. The brush-traces in a composition may be far fewer than what is seen in a Northern Sung painting, but the empty spaces resonate with a lively, palpable atmosphere. By cutting away this small scene for our perusal, the artist's approach of selecting scenery to create a realm becomes richer and the variations on the painting surface become more plentiful.

Although Su Shih wrote that to discuss painting in terms of formal likeness is to show the understanding of a child, Sung painting can be discussed in terms of formal likeness. Yüan painting, on the other hand, is something different. The landscapes that the Yüan painters create pass first through the "heart's eye" before flowing forth to paper or silk. A world is created, complete and all its own, within which one finds lodged the painter's thoughts and ideals. If one approaches Yüan dynasty landscape with a standard of photographic realism, then one will certainly be disappointed, but if one looks at Yüan painting as the expression of human thoughts and feelings, then the landscape becomes something sublime and elegant. Yüan painting marks a great expansion of the small-scale meeting of emotion and scene that we find in the Southern Sung.

Painting styles of both the Ming and Ch'ing dynasties received the influences of Sung and Yüan. The high achievements established by these two earlier epochs set a precedent and standard. They provided models that could be emulated, with the consequence that the experience of true landscape became less of a factor in the making of paintings. On paper or silk, it is the painter who now masters nature. The illusionistic handling of space becomes less of a priority, as layer after layer of constructed scenery appears.

The transformation between Sung and Yüan painting seems remarkably pronounced and yet the formation of a painting style is not something that takes place in a day and night; nor is it something that can be simply explained by a change of dynasties. Although there was a reaction against Southern Sung painting in the early years of the Yüan, the models to which some turned were of the Northern Sung. For example, the emphasis of both composition and form that one sees in Northern Sung bird-and-flower painting is also visible in the finely detailed work of such Yüan painters as Ch'ien Hsüan and

Wang Yüan. Moreover, in landscape painting, one finds the strong influence of Li Ch'eng and Kuo Hsi, whose styles merge in the Yüan dynasty to form the basis of the so-called Li-Kuo school. Not only are these landscapes composed with the grand scale and breadth of vision associated with the earlier painters' work, motifs are emulated and repeated as well. Chao Meng-fu spent some time and energy learning this style of painting and there were others who specialized in it, such as T'ang Ti, Ts'ao Chih-po and Chu Te-jun. Through the Southern Sung, painters of the Imperial Painting Academy reigned supreme. In the Yüan, their place of importance is taken over by a rising tide of literati painters. This also can be recognized as a return to the Northern Sung, to the path first forged by Su Shih, Wen T'ung, Li Kung-lin and others. The literati tradition of painting, blocked by the Southern Sung, is picked up again in the Yüan dynasty. Its energy would rarely falter through the later history of Chinese painting.

130 Li K'an, Yüan dynasty: Bamboo Branches.

Chapter Five

The Ming Dynasty
1368~1644

1. The Re-establishment of Court Painting

With the founding of the Ming dynasty, the system of governance established in the earlier native Chinese dynasties of T'ang and Sung was resurrected. The Ming court re-established an imperial painting academy. In scale and institutional authority, it could not compare with the formal organization of the Sung, but the Ming painting academy still attracted considerable talent. The Hsüan-te (1426-35), Ch'eng-hua (1465-87) and Hung-chih (1488-1504) reigns were the most active periods of the Ming imperial academy. Emperor Hsüan-tsung (r. 1425-35) himself was an excellent painter, skilled in particular in bird-and-flower and animal subjects. His painting such as "Gibbons at Play" (fig. 132), while not quite up to the exceptional standards of Sung Hui-tsung, has artistic merit well beyond the kinds of paintings that are preserved simply because the painter happened to be an important historical figure. Hsüan-tsung was also important for helping to foster a high standard of achievement among the court artists.

Perhaps the earliest distinctive Ming court painter to emerge was Pien Wen-chin (ca. 1354- ca. 1428) whose paintings are infused with the rich, warm color harmonies that typify the palace style. His paintings of bird-and-flower subjects, represented here by "Three Friends and One Hundred Birds" (fig. 133), utilize the compositional principles of the T'ang and Sung traditions, if perhaps lacking a bit of the intricate detail and tightness evident in a good Sung dynasty painting. Succeeding Pien Wen-chin in the field of bird-and-flower painting was the Hung-chih reign period artist Lü Chi. Lü Chi was even more persistent in chasing after the Sung dynasty style, but he added novel elements to his paintings, as well as a romantic air. "Water Fowl on an Islet in Autumn" (fig. 134) shows Lü Chi's remarkable ability to present the tactile character of the birds' plumage. Offset by heavy mists, the birds present a rich, dazzling image of elegance and beauty. A less restrained form of bird-and-flower painting, utilizing only ink and inkwash, was also practiced at the Ming painting academy by the artist Lin Liang (ca. 1416- ca. 1480). The excellence of Lin Liang's dripping style, which shared common characteristics with works by contemporary painters of the Che school, is well demonstrated in his paintings of such subjects as peacocks and eagles (fig. 135).

2. The Unfettered Che School

Towards the end of the Yüan dynasty and in the early years of the Ming, a number of prominent literati painters became involved in political activities, oftentimes with disastrous results. While this represented a temporary lull in the development of literati painting, another school, which emulated the inkwash styles of the Southern Sung academy painters Ma Yüan and Hsia Kuei, came to the fore. The Che school, as the group came to be known after the geographical affiliation with the Chekiang region of Tai Chin (1388-1462) (fig. 27), the school's most prominent figure, added vigor and daring to the subtlety of the

131 T'ang Yin, Ming dynasty:
Hermit Fishermen in Streams and Mountains
(detail).

173

132 Emperor Hsüan-tsung, Ming dynasty:
Gibbons at Play.

134 Lü Chi, Ming dynasty:
Water Fowl on an Islet in Autumn.

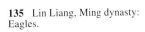

135 Lin Liang, Ming dynasty:
Eagles.

Left
133 Pien Wen-Chin, Ming dynasty:
Three Friends and One Hundred Birds.

136 Wu Wei, Ming dynasty:
The Joy of Fishermen (detail).

137 Wang E, Ming dynasty:
Auspicious Snow of Frozen Winter (detail).

Southern Sung academy painters. The Ma-Hsia style of landscape painting had continued to be practiced in Hangchou and northern Chekiang through the fourteenth century, but now it was recast into a dramatic display of powerful ax-cut texturing strokes, boldly contrastive layers of inkwash and thick atmospheric effects. The resulting tone was especially well-suited to themes that emphasized dramatic momentary impressions, such as a boat returning in a sudden rainstorm. Che school artists often painted historical narratives and realistic images of the common people, such as fishing families in their daily activities (fig. 136).

The Che school's activity peaked during the period of Tai Chin's activity to the Hung-chih and Cheng-te reigns. It was encouraged by patronage from the court in Beijing. The painter Wu Wei (1459-1508), for example, was bestowed the title Principal Graduate of Painting and another painter named Wang E (active ca. 1462-1541) was honored as "today's Ma Yüan" (fig. 137).

Although the Che school emulated the styles of Ma Yüan and Hsia Kuei, their method of presention was something considerably different from what had appeared in the thirteenth century. Ma Yüan's and Hsia Kuei's styles remained fundamentally rooted in an attitude that sought to present the reality of nature. By the Ming dynasty, however, the artists' orientation had shifted from nature to earlier paintings. The practice of learning by copying earlier works strengthened, and the expert handling of spatial depth that is the hallmark of Sung landscapes disappears. The artist, one could say, becomes most interested in displaying himself. The paintings are often large, with the atrical details for increasing the visual interest. Comparing Ma Yüan's and Hsia Kuei's work (figs. 16, 21, 111) with the work of Tai Chin and Wu Wei (figs. 27, 136), we note how these Ming masters were still able to exhibit the intrinsic interest of brush and ink. By the late phase of Che school painting, however, technique becomes overly emphasized and the paintings sometimes succumb to a rash display of untempered ink-play. Subtlety and lofty transcendence are lost, leading to the pejorative label "the wild and heterodox school."

3. The Cultured Wu School

Already in the Ming dynasty there are various references to a group of painters collectively known as the Wu school. Wu specifically refers to the city and environs of Suchou in Kiangsu Province. The Wu school designates painters active in a triangular area between Suchou and Lake T'ai. During the Ch'eng-hua reign period, the Suchou painter Shen Chou (1427-1509) helped reinvigorate the tradition of literati painting that had blossomed in this general area during the Yüan. Born to a family with a scholarly background, Shen Chou added diligence to his natural talent in painting, so that ultimately he became adept at all of the major subjects— landscape, figures and birds-and-flowers. His landscape painting was modeled after Tung Yüan and Chü-jan, to whose styles he added the four masters of the Yüan (Huang Kung-wang, Wu Chen, Ni Tsan and Wang Meng). His early painting was delicate, refined and light. After the age of fifty, he pursued a clean and abrupt style associated with the Southern Sung painters, employing darkly toned ink and a coarse brush. In his late years, he shifted again, this time turning to Wu Chen, the Two Mis (Mi Fu and Mi Yu-jen) and Kao K'o-kung. One could say that Shen Chou spent his entire artistic life shifting between Sung and Yüan. Outwardly, his paintings present the quiet calm of Yüan, but the underlying bone-structure is strong and stable, like Sung (figs. 66, 138).

Beginning in the Yüan dynasty, the Suchou area became a center for painting. Much of the city's fame in this regard was owed to Shen Chou, whose accomplishments were widely celebrated. Immediately following Shen Chou and counted as his disciples are the excellent painters Wen Cheng-ming and T'ang Yin. Wen Cheng-ming lived to be almost ninety and he himself nurtured a number of excellent artists, including his sons Wen Chia and Wen P'eng, his nephew Wen Po-jen and his students Ch'en Ch'un, Lu Chih and Ch'ien Ku.

Another notable painter of the sixteenth century was Ch'iu Ying, who hailed from nearby T'ai-ts'ang. Although his style of painting was not directly learned from Wen Cheng-ming, Ch'iu Ying was socially active in Suchou's literati circles. The congregation of all of this talent in Suchou naturally led to comparisons with the Che school painters and the Wu school was born.

Wen Cheng-ming (1470-1559) learned directly from Shen Chou and his work reveals a close relationship. His early painting is characterized by brushwork that is clean, taut and slender. His landscape paintings in the blue-green style, as well as paintings of figures and orchids (fig. 28), adopted the styles of Chao Meng-fu, while his landscapes with light colors and inkwash resemble those of the Yüan painter Wang Meng. In his late years, Wen Cheng-ming's work became especially strong and energetic, as proven by "Old Trees by a Cold Stream" (fig. 64).

Joining Shen Chou and Wen Cheng-ming as the Four Masters of the Ming are T'ang Yin and Ch'iu Ying. T'ang Yin (1470-1523) studied with Shen Chou. Ch'iu Ying (ca. 1494- ca.1552) had frequent contacts with the Wen family. Because both T'ang Yin and Ch'iu Ying also studied painting with the professional painter Chou Ch'en, they are also sometimes labeled members of the academic or professional school. T'ang Yin was born in the same year as Wen Cheng-ming and his early painting is rather close in style. Later, however, T'ang Yin studied the Sung landscape artists Li T'ang and Kuo Hsi, and his painting consequently presented an image of heroic strength. While this led to a pronounced

138 Shen Chou, Ming dynasty: Lofty Mount Lu. (detail *right*)

女几山前野路横 松聲偏稱合泉聲

靜裏間傾耳便覺沖然道氣生

李父母大人先生 治下唐寅畫呈

139 T'ang Yin, Ming dynasty: Soughing Pines on a Mountain Path.　(detail *left*)

140 Ch'en Ch'un,
Ming dynasty:
Flowers.

141 Ch'en Hung-shou, Ming dynasty: Rock of Inebriation.

departure from the styles of Shen Chou and Wen Cheng-ming, T'ang Yin's lofty, elegant air nonetheless shares much in common with the other Wu school painters (figs. 48, 131, 139). Ch'iu Ying was active during the Cheng-te and Chia-ching reigns (1506-66). In his youth he worked as a lacquer craftsman. Mastering painting, he developed a highly refined, precise and richly colored style that earned high praise (fig. 1). Ch'iu Ying was a multi-talented painter adept at all styles and subjects. It was unusual for a painter who was not of a scholarly background to receive the wide esteem that Ch'iu Ying enjoyed, but this can be taken as a measure of his skill. The long-lived Chou Ch'en is another painter who was active in sixteenth century Suchou. His influence on T'ang Yin and Ch'iu Ying should not be underestimated. Chou Ch'en's style of landscape painting is close to that of T'ang Yin.

4. The Untamed Style of Bird-and-Flower and Figure Painting

Monochrome ink painting of bird-and-flower subjects reveal some new developments in the Ming dynasty. Lin Liang, mentioned earlier, offers one example (fig. 135). Slightly before him, Wang Fu and Hsia Ch'ang were well-known for their bamboo painting. Shen Chou presents yet another new development. His paintings of flowers, fruits, birds and animals, painted with strong brushwork and colors, present something entirely different from the calm, peaceful atmosphere of Yüan painting.

After Shen Chou, there were painters whose individual styles were even more pronounced, such as Ch'en Ch'un and Hsü Wei. Ch'en Ch'un (1484-1544) studied under Wen Cheng-ming but succeeded in breaking out of the mold established by his teacher. His painting style belongs to the category of *hsieh-i*, or "the sketching of one's ideas," though within the direct expression of his feelings and ideas appear rules and methods—a touch of delicacy within the coarseness (fig. 140). With Hsü Wei, feelings and ideas are allowed to tumble forth in a bold display of magnificent unrestraint. His painting of grapes, introduced in a previous chapter, well demonstrates the overflowing charm of his ink (fig. 46). Ch'en Chun and Hsü Wei, often grouped together, become the patriarchs for later painters of plants and flowers in the *hsieh-i* mode.

At the very end of the Ming dynasty, Ch'en Hung-shou (1598-1652) established a new form of figure painting, which can be summed up by the single word "bizarre." The peculiarly modeled heads of his figures are overly large in proportion to bodies which are unbalanced, yet Ch'en Hung-shou's characters possess tremendous personality and expression. They transport the viewer to a world that is at once lofty, archaic and totally removed from common experience (fig. 141). Ting Yun-p'eng and Wu Pin painted figures that were equally unusual.

5. The Theory of the Northern and Southern Schools

Towards the end of the Ming dynasty, Tung Ch'i-ch'ang (1555-1636) formulated his theory of the Northern and Southern Schools of landscape painting, a theory that has dominated thinking about Chinese painting for more than three hundred years. It is only within the last few decades that art historians have dared to challenge Tung Ch'i-ch'ang's ideas by pointing out certain inconsistencies. Regardless of how valid or invalid Tung's theory of the Northern and Southern Schools is, it remains important to understand. The following passage from Tung Ch'i-ch'ang's writings will introduce it:

In Ch'an (Zen) Buddhism, two diverging schools began to develop in the T'ang dynasty: the Northern and Southern. In painting there are also a Northern and a Southern school and these too first emerged in the T'ang dynasty. The Northern School of painting began with Li Ssu-hsün's polychrome landscapes. It was later transmitted to Chao Kan, Chao Po-chü and Chao Po-su of the Sung dynasty, and then to Ma Yüan, Hsia Kuei and their generation. As for the Southern School, it began with Wang Wei's inkwash painting, which completely transformed the detailed, outline approach. His lineage was continued by Chang Ts'ao, Ching Hao, Kuan T'ung, Kuo Chung-shu, Tung Yüan, Chü-jan, Mi Fu and son Mi Yu-jen, and the four masters of the Yüan. Just as it is with the later generations of the six schools of Ch'an Buddhism, (the Southern School) has flourished like the followers of (the Ch'an sects) Ma-chu, Yun-men and Lin-ch'i, while the Northern School has declined.

Tung Ch'i-ch'ang defines the characterisitics of the two lineages of painting. Moreover, he directly states that the Southern School has flourished while the Northern School has faltered. In fact, Southern School really refers to the literati painting that develops during the Yüan dynasty.

Tung Ch'i-ch'ang's own landscape painting, exemplified by "Discussing Connoisseurship at Feng-ching" (fig. 142), pursues that element of substantiality that one finds in Sung painting. Even more important is his development of a kind of abstract space, one in which there is no emphasis of layering and depth. In fact, his landscape paintings can be considered as a manner of abstract painting. It was extremely influential on later developments in the genre.

Between the Sung and Yüan dynasties and the Ming and Ch'ing dynasties appeared two major figures in Chinese painting: Chao Meng-fu and Tung Ch'i-ch'ang. By coincidence, both of these painters were posthumously named Wen-min, and both were tremendously influential on the painting that immediately followed them. Chao Meng-fu forged a new beginning for painting in the Yüan. Tung Ch'i-ch'ang held important official positions and he became a creative leader for painters of his time. His student Wang Shih-min, for example, later became a leading figure as one of the six masters of the early Ch'ing and a representative of the school of orthodox painting whose roots were deeply connected to Tung Ch'i-ch'ang's painting. Moreover, even the individualists of the early Ch'ing such as Shih-t'ao and Pa-ta shan-jen were in many ways indebted to Tung Ch'i-ch'ang's innovations. From this, one can measure Tung Ch'i-ch'ang's importance to Ch'ing dynasty painting. In addition, Tung Ch'i-ch'ang was an extremely influential theoretician. He elevated literati painting to a position of unparalleled status, thus insuring its place of singular importance in the history of Chinese painting. In this regard, Tung Ch'i-ch'ang's contributions will never be erased. It matters little if Tung Ch'i-ch'ang's theories do not always meet with approval today. In the least, people pay attention to what he had to say.

Tung Ch'i-ch'ang's Lineages

1. The Northern School:
Colored landscapes (referring to the blue-green and gold-green styles). Using a detailed outline method of description.
2. The Southern School:
Inkwash landscapes.
Tonal colors of ink form the basis for description.

142 Tung Ch'i-ch'ang, Ming dynasty: Discussing Connoisseurship at Feng-Ching.

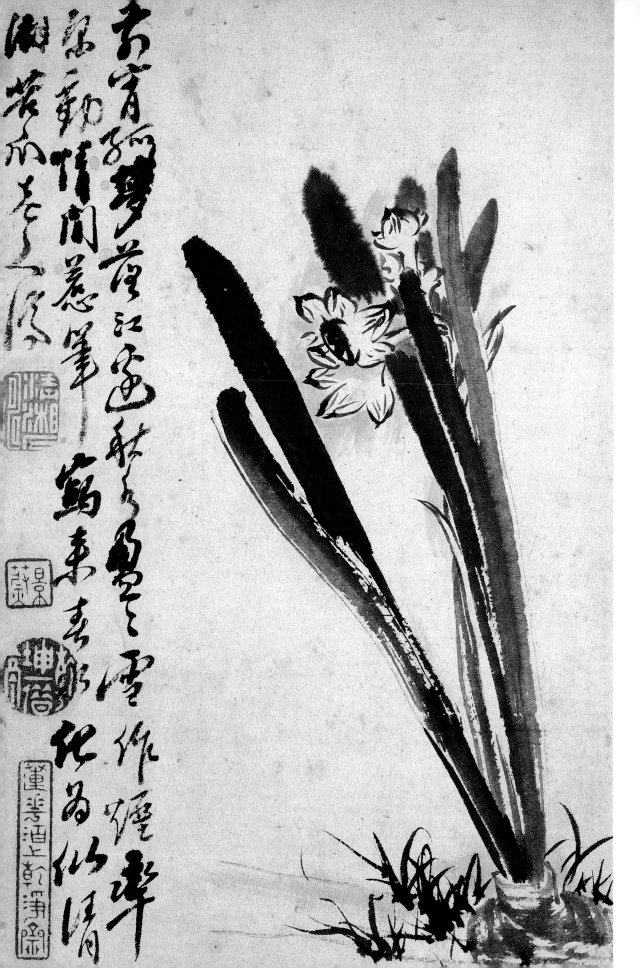

Chapter Six
The Ch'ing Dynasty
1644~1911

1. The Orthodox School: Landscapes of the Four Wangs, Wu and Yun

A number of painters of the early Ch'ing dynasty upheld and continued the tradition of literati painting that had evolved from the Yüan and Ming dynasties. In approach and technique they were heavily influenced by the teachings of Tung Ch'i-ch'ang. The prevailing trend at the time was to honor the painters of Tung Ch'i-ch'ang's Southern School. From this evolved a practice of modeling one's painting after the styles of earlier masters and of creating within parameters defined by the paintings of the ancients. Representative of this kind of painting are Wang Shih-min (fig. 144), Wang Chien (fig. 145), Wang Hui (fig. 146), Wang Yüan-ch'i (fig. 147), Wu Li (fig. 149) and Yun Shou-p'ing (fig. 148), who have been collectively called the six great masters of the early Ch'ing.

Wang Shih-min (1592-1680) personally received the teachings of Tung Ch'i-ch'ang and he considered himself Tung's true follower. Wang Chien (1598-1677) did not directly study with Tung Ch'i-ch'ang, but he too pursued the routes of the Sung and Yüan masters. As Wang Chien's adoption of traditional styles was precisely the same as Wang Shih-min's, there is a close similarity in their styles. In his youth, Wang Hui (1632-1720) received the attention and training of these two older Wangs, Wang Shih-min and Wang Chien, and he carried forth the orthodox teachings by melding all of the various styles of the Southern School into a great synthesis. Wang Yüan-ch'i (1642-1715), the grandson of Wang Shih-min, was deeply immersed in the family's tradition of study and art. Wu Li (1632-1718) established a somewhat independent style from the four Wangs, but he too was originally a disciple of Wang Shih-min. Yun Shou-p'ing's (1633-90) reputation soared as a painter of plants and flowers (figs. 38, 44). Although he painted landscapes as well, Yun Shou-p'ing purposely chose to specialize in flower painting in order to avoid a potential conflict with his friend Wang Hui whose forte was landscape painting. Yun Shou-p'ing's approach to painting practice and theory shared the four Wangs' inheritance of Tung Ch'i-ch'ang's legacy. These six masters established one important school of painting in the early Ch'ing. Its influence was deep and longlasting.

The painting of the six masters has its foundations in *lin-mo* or "copying." One studies the ancient masters by copying the paintings that one encounters. Each stroke and dot has its source in an earlier work. From this disciplined course of study, one intuits the enlightened spirit of the ancients. One's foundation is thus established in the wisdom of antiquity, combining the strengths of the many to arrive eventually at the pinnacle of creativity. Too often the term *lin-mo* is mistaken to mean halting at the process of imitating earlier painters, limiting one's styles and subjects and thus losing the precious freedom of creativity that is the basis of art. To outward appearances it seems this way, especially as many of these artists' paintings, including those illustrated here, speak of copying the brush-mode of one master or another. These paintings, however, are not rigid imitations of earlier artists' work. Take Wang Yüan-ch'i as an example. Many times he painted landscapes which he claimed were after Huang Kung-wang's "Autumn Mountains," yet in his lifetime he never saw the original painting

143 Shih-t'ao, Ch'ing dynasty: Album of Flowers.

144 Wang Shih-min, Ch'ing dynasty: After Wang Wei's "Clearing Snow on the River".

145 Wang Chien, Ch'ing dynasty: After a Landscape by Chao Meng-fu.

石谷此畫雅做山樵而用筆措
思令人石必惫宗故風肎高奇迥
出山樵規格之外春晚通景雄以
見際余知欲昌之知其意頗自除不
恐返奢每展懷一觇余待方岩嫩
浮此飽紀黑日雀熙夫雨所在始
知昔人椒愈頗風良不厝也
庚戌釟雨後一日西廬夫人王博故題

146 Wang Hui, Ch'ing dynasty:
Mountains, Streams and Autumn-tinted Trees.

甲戌初秋做李熊山樵夏
日山居圖筆意
王原祁

147 Wang Yüan-ch'i, Ch'ing dynasty: Living in the Mountains in Summer.

148 Yun Shou-p'ing, Ch'ing dynasty:
Old Trees and Bamboo in the Style of Ni Tsan.

149 Wu Li, Ch'ing dynasty:
After a Landscape by Wu Chen (detail).

once. This approach to painting is called "borrowing the wine goblet of another to irrigate the rocky terrain of one's own breast." The six masters' imitation of earlier styles was an attempt to ressurect the idealized methods of antiquity. What they pursued was not a formal duplication of what had already been done, but rather a spiritual communion with those artists who had already been lionized as the finest in the history of Chinese painting.

2. The Individualism of the Loyalist Painters

In contrast to the orthodoxy of the Four Wangs, Wu Li and Yun Shou-p'ing, a number of painters active in the second half of the seventeenth century emphasized a more individualistic and self-expressive approach. These include Shih-hsi (K'un-ts'an), Chien-chiang (Hung-jen), Pa-ta shan-jen, Shih-t'ao, Mei Ch'ing and Kung Hsien. Chien-chiang's (1610-1664) style of painting is refined, pristine and simplified. His landscapes, represented by "Pines and Rocks of the Yellow Sea" (fig. 2, discussed in Chapter One), present a world that is bright and clean. Kung Hsien (ca. 1619-89) was Chien-chiang's precise opposite. His compelling landscape "A Thousand Cliffs and Myriad Ravines" (fig. 49) is built of thick layers of dark, mysterious ink coupled with occasional passages of thread-like luminosity. The result is another dream-like world, though one far removed from Chien-chiang's open realm of light and air. Shih-t'ao's (1642-1707?) paintings often display a wet inkwash technique (fig. 143). He carved a seal that reads, "Scouring the earth in search of strange peaks for my painting drafts" (fig. 69.1) and his landscapes do justice to this unusual claim (fig. 150). With his extraordinarily varied compositions, Shih-t'ao ranks as one of the greatest of all Chinese landscape painters. Mei Ch'ing's (1623-97) style of painting is rather similar to the work of Shih-t'ao, with an added element of loftiness (fig. 4). Shih-hsi's (1612-74) landscapes are remarkably dense, strong and unpolished. They give the impression of a rough farmer with uncombed hair who pays little attention to his appearance. Nonetheless, his paintings possess a strong spirit that is readily conveyed (fig. 151). The individualism of these artists is well presented in the following comment by Shih-t'ao:

> The whiskers and eyebrows of the ancients do not grow on my face, and their lungs and bowels cannot enter my breast. I give vent to my own lungs and bowels, and I present my own whiskers and brows. If at some time my paintings happen to bear resemblance to those of some other fellow, it is he who copies me. I do not try to be him.

In the painting of our own century, there has been a marked emphasis on individual creativity and for this reason artists such as Shih-t'ao and Pa-ta shan-jen have received particular favor. The preceding discussion has emphasized the landscapes of these painters to contrast with those of the orthodox school, but their achievements were not limited to this subject. Pa-ta shan-jen's paintings of birds, flowers and fish, and Shih-t'ao's cymbidiums and bamboo all represent outstanding achievements. The bold inkwash painters of earlier in the Ming dynasty, such as Shen Chou and Ch'en Ch'un, painted in styles that remained well within the boundaries of proper rules and methods. With Hsü Wei, painting began to loosen up; feelings come pouring out onto the paper with nothing left in reserve. With Pa-ta shan-jen, however, there is another transformation. His flowers and birds, so carefully created and arranged, sometimes seem overly exaggerated, yet they possess their own particular spirit, forged from

150 Shih-t'ao, Ch'ing dynasty:
Gazing at the Waterfall on Mount Lu.

151 Shih-hsi, Ch'ing dynasty:
Tall Mountains, Long Rivers.

tremendous concentration (fig. 45). Pa-ta's ink at first seems to have been wielded with great abandon, but a closer look reveals masterful control and an element of subtlety and restraint. Shih-t'ao's spirited rendering of blossoming plum, cymbidiums, bamboo and narcissus (fig. 143) give the impression of a young handsome man standing in the wind. One can hardly speak about early Ch'ing dynasty flower painting without also mentioning Yun Shou-p'ing. Within the graceful brushwork of his "boneless" style of painting flowers (figs. 38, 44) emerges an irresistable freshness and purity.

3. Influence from the West

In the fifteenth and sixteenth centuries, traders and missionaries from the west risked their lives on the long, perilous journey to China. Some of them carried works of art. In this manner, European painting was introduced to China. The most famous of the Jesuits was Matteo Ricci (1552-1610), who traveled to the Ming dynasty capital at Beijing in 1601 and presented an image of the Virgin and Child to Emperor Shen-tsung. Ricci established a church and raised an image of Jesus within the church. He also used Western style pictures to illustrate stories from the Bible, thus allowing Chinese to become familiar with this foreign mode of pictorial description. People of the time thought extremely highly of these images. The Virgin Mary, for example, was described as possessing eyebrows, eyes and garment folds as clear as if one were looking in a mirror. Such lifelike images with clearly rendered expressions seemed beyond the reach of Chinese painters. The buildings looked like they could be entered directly; relative distances appeared precisely calculated, all just as in real life.

How was it that these painted images could appear so lifelike, with bodies and limbs that seemed to swell right out from within the canvas? The answer, of course, lay with the European artist's emphasis of light, its changing patterns and effects on objects, and the technique of chiaroscuro, which greatly heightened the three-dimensional quality of the images, especially when contrasted with the Chinese painter's flat application of colors and emphasis on overall atmosphere. As for the illusionism of the buildings in the Western paintings, this stemmed from the painters' faithful use of principles of visual perspective and an exacting maintenance of proper scale. We are all perfectly familiar with these characteristics of Western painting today, but three to four hundred years ago they seemed utterly novel to Chinese viewers and far removed from what was emphasized in Chinese painting.

In the end, there were not many Chinese painters who adopted the Western methods of rendering light and perspective. In figure painting, the most notable was the Ming dynasty painter Tseng Ching from Fukien Province. Tseng Ching changed the traditional method of painting faces with flat planes by building various layers of color and shading to bring out all of the subtle modeling of his subjects. His manner of painting was carried forward by his disciples to become one important stream of figure painting in late traditional China. Tseng Ching's influence can still be seen in many anonymous ancestral portraits. The Western style of rendering light, however, raised a serious problem for the Chinese. In Western painting, the tone of a color is determined by the amount of light that illuminates a particular area of the painting. Under a fixed light source, a three-dimensional object will possess both light and dark areas. The lit areas would be painted with bright colors, while the unlit areas would remain shaded and dark, painted with dim colors or even black. The principle is the same for the painting of faces, but the Chinese painter and viewer found it difficult to accept this, as it gave the subject an inauspicious aura. In the worst case, a shadow rendered on the face with a bit of black might make it seem that the figure had died. For this reason, although a Chinese painting would possess different gradations of tone, this tonal range would appear within a single color. This was the only way that modeling was found acceptable to the Chinese viewer.

The influence of Western painting was most notable with painters active at the early Ch'ing dynasty court. This was due to the presence of Giuseppe Castiglione (Lang Shih-ning, 1688-1766) (fig. 152) and a few other missionary painters, who found the best avenue for expanding their religious activities was to earn the emperor's appreciation for foreign skills such as painting. There were other westerners happy to introduce Western painting techniques to court painters and high officials who were employed at the Ch'ing court's Directorate of Astronomy. For these reasons, painters at the court had many more opportunities to see and learn directly from Western painting than those on the outside. The most notable Chinese painter to adopt Western techniques was Chiao Ping-chen, a skilled mathematician employed

152 Lang Shih-ning, Ch'ing dynasty: Album of Flower Paintings.

at the Directorate of Astronomy. Chiao Ping-chen's contacts with westerners at the court led him to the methods of Western style perspective.

4. The Eccentrics of Yangchou

During the Ch'ien-lung reign (1736-96), the Grand Canal city of Yangchou (Kiangsu Province) became a major economic center. Prosperity from the flourishing salt trade and silk industry helped support the arts, leading to the congregation of a number of painters here. A new movement in Chinese painting took place under these conditions, represented by a group of artists collectively known as the Eight Eccentrics of Yangchou. Which eight artists comprise the Eight Eccentrics, however, is a matter of some debate, as the following nine names appear in different sources: Cheng Hsieh (Cheng Pan-ch'iao), Li Shan (ca. 1686- before 1765), Chin Nung (1687-1763) (fig. 156), Lo P'ing (1733-99) (fig. 154), Li Fang-ying, Huang Shen (1686- ca. 1766), Kao Hsiang, Wang Shih-shen (1686-1759) and Hua Yen (1682- ca. 1765) (fig. 153). Two other figures, Min Chen and Kao Feng-han (1683-1749) (fig. 155), are also often added and some remove Li Fang-ying from the list, as his activity may have been centered in Nanking rather than Yangchou. All of these artists sold paintings for a living in Yangchou, but they were not professional painters in the traditional sense. Rather, they were educated men, literati, well versed in the world of letters and poetry. Moreover, some served as high officials. The well-known Cheng Hsieh, for example, was a district magistrate in Shantung Province and Li Shan served at the court before losing interest and retiring to make a living as a painter. All of these men were also excellent calligraphers and they developed personal styles quite removed from the orthodox modes practiced in the world of officialdom. The Yangchou eccentrics largely specialized in the subjects of plum blossoms, cymbidiums, bamboo, chrysanthemums, the cursive manner of sketching birds and flowers, and figures. The most important characteristic of their paintings is the expression of an individual manner and a direct, uninhibited revelation of ideas and feelings. Close to their own time, they were influenced by Shih-t'ao and Pa-ta shan-jen. More distantly, the sources for their art included Shen Chou, Ch'en Ch'un and Hsü Wei. Although grouped together, each of these painters had his own individual style. The hallmark of the Yangchou eccentrics was a talent for presenting one's own personality.

Landscape painting after the Ch'ien-lung reign period declined in energy and creativity while the cursive sketching of bird-and-flower subjects became a favorite mode of painting of most of the later masters. This phenomenon is largely owed to the influence of the Yangchou eccentrics. Chin Nung's painting, for example, overflows with the simple, unpolished aesthetic of the antiquarian *chin-shih* ("metal and stone" or epigraphy) movement (fig. 156). His weighty, substantial style of painting strongly influenced the late Ch'ing and early twentieth century painters Chao Chih-ch'ien, Wu Ch'ang-shih and Ch'i P'ai-shih, who are now collectively known as masters of the Metal and Stone School. Similarly, the cursive manner of sketching bird-and-flower painting practiced by Kao Feng-han, Li Shan, Huang Shen and Li Fang-ying was the inspiration for the art of Wu Hsi-tsai, Chao Chih-ch'ien, Jen Po-nien, Wu Ch'ang-shih, Ch'en Shih-tseng and Ch'i Pai-shih, and a number of Fukien painters were influenced by the figure painting styles of Huang Shen and Min Chen.

In certain respects, the Yangchou eccentrics exemplify the essential character of literati painting. By literati standards, an artist's education and upbringing figure into the critique of his work, which means that training in

153 Hua Yen, Ch'ing dynasty: The Piled Snows of T'ien-shan.

poetry and calligraphy are expected, and the ability to combine these two together with painting: the "three excellences." These criteria are certainly fulfilled by the Yangchou eccentrics' work. Moreover, looking at their paintings today, it seems less eccentric than one might expect. Nonetheless, by traditional standards, their paintings offered something unusual. It combined the three excellences of literati painting, but it did not adopt the posture of a lofty disinterest in material gain that was once an essential element in defining the scholar's role as a painter. The Yangchou eccentrics all sold paintings to make a living. At the same time, their paintings, filled with energy and life, do not reveal the professional painter's concern for the market.

In today's industrial society, flourishing economic centers often provide the spark for lively art movements. Eighteenth century Yangchou with its salt trade was followed by nineteenth century Shanghai, a center for international transport. Taipei today is no different. In this regard, the Yangchou eccentrics set the way for the emergence of the modern artist. After them a professionalized literati painting formally emerges. Perhaps this is the real reason for their "eccentric" label.

154 Lo P'ing, Ch'ing dynasty: Portrait of I-an.

155 Kao Feng-han, Ch'ing dynasty: Peonies.

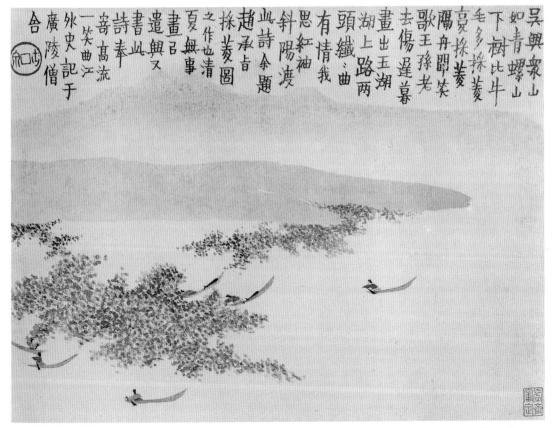

156 Chin Nung, Ch'ing dynasty: Picking Water-chestnuts.

5. The Metal and Stone School and the Shanghai School

The Ch'ien-lung and Chia-ch'ing reign periods witnessed the blossoming of a new school of study based on careful examination of historical facts and sources. Particular attention was drawn to archaic bronze ritual vessels and stone engravings that were unearthed and researched, which broadened the scope of this new tide of learning to include calligraphy. It led to a growing appreciation for the strong, bold style of writing that was found on stelae of the Northern Wei period. In the nineteenth century, calligraphers such as Wu Hsi-tsai and Chao Chih-ch'ien not only excelled at the study of stelae, they were also talented seal carvers and they carried their mature calligraphic skills over to painting. Their paintings possess a refreshing, natural air and an element of the strength that characterizes Northern Wei calligraphy. Combining the three excellences of earlier literati painting with compositional and aesthetic qualities learned from seal carving, these painters became known as the Metal and Stone School. Chao Chih-ch'ien (1829-84) is the most important (fig. 157). In the album leaf chosen to present his art, we note both the richness of his conception and the maturity of his brushwork. Wu Ch'ang-shih (fig. 73) and Ch'i Pai-shih (figs. 50, 69.4), two of the great masters of relatively recent times, were both late adherents of the school who excelled at the three arts of calligraphy, painting and seal carving.

157 Chao Chih-ch'ien, Ch'ing dynasty: Album of Flowers.

After the Opium War, Shanghai became the economic center of China and painters from all over the country gathered to sell their work. Collectively they are known as the Shanghai School, though their styles of painting, in fact, are not necessarily related. Jen Po-nien (Jen I) (1840-95) was one of the more important figures (fig. 158). He modeled his figure painting after the work of the late Ming dynasty artist Ch'en Hung-shou, but his talents extended to just about every subject. As a professional, Jen Po-nien produced a large body of work, but it was without the stiff, meticulous manners that sometimes discolor professional painting.

158 Jen I, Ch'ing dynasty: Wisteria, Bamboo and Narcissus.

■ List of Plates

112 Su Han-ch'en, Sung dynasty:
Children Playing in the Autumn Garden.
The National Palace Museum, Taipei.

113 Liu Sung-nien, Sung dynasty:
Lohan (Arhat).
The National Palace Museum, Taipei.

114 Ma Ho-chih, Sung dynasty:
Ancient Tree by Flowing Water.
The National Palace Museum, Taipei.

115 Li Sung, Sung dynasty:
Village Peddler with Playing Children.
The National Palace Museum, Taipei.

116 Liang K'ai, Sung dynasty:
Li Po Chanting a Poem while Strolling.
Tokyo National Museum.

117 Mu-ch'i, Sung dynasty:
Six Persimmons.
Daitoku-ji, Kyoto.

118 Shih K'o, Five dynasties period:
The Two Patriarchs Harmonizing Their Minds.
Tokyo National Museum.

119, 121 Chao Meng-fu, Yüan dynasty:
Autumn Colors on the Ch'üeh and Hua Mountains.
The National Palace Museum, Taipei.

120 Liu Kuan-tao, Yüan dynasty:
Whiling away the Summer.
The Nelson-Atkins Museum of Art, Kansas City.

123 Wu Chen, Yüan dynasty:
Hermit Fisherman on Lake Tung-t'ing.
The National Palace Museum, Taipei.

125 Wang Meng, Yüan dynasty:
Lin-wu Grotto at Chü-ch'ü.
The National Palace Museum, Taipei.

126 Kung K'ai, Yüan dynasty:
Emaciated Horse.
Osaka Municipal Museum.

127 Cheng Ssu-hsiao, Yüan dynasty:
Orchid.
Osaka Municipal Museum.

128 Wang Yüan, Yüan dynasty:
Birds, Bamboo and Rock.
Shanghai Museum.

129 Yen Hui, Yüan dynasty:
Drunken Immortal.
Lan-ch'ien shan-kuan, Taipei.

130 Li K'an, Yüan dynasty:
Bamboo Branches.
The National Palace Museum, Taipei.

131 T'ang Yin, Ming dynasty:
Hermit Fishermen in Streams and Mountains.
The National Palace Museum, Taipei.

132 Emperor Hsüan-tsung, Ming dynasty:
Gibbons at Play.
The National Palace Museum, Taipei.

133 Pien Wen-chin, Ming dynasty:
Three Friends and One Hundred Birds.
The National Palace Museum, Taipei.

134 Lü Chi, Ming dynasty:
Water Fowl on an Islet in Autumn.
The National Palace Museum, Taipei.

135 Lin Liang, Ming dynasty:
Eagles.
The National Palace Museum, Taipei.

136 Wu Wei, Ming dynasty:
The Joy of Fishermen.
Private collection.

137 Wang E, Ming dynasty:
Auspicious Snow of Frozen Winter.
The National Palace Museum, Taipei.

138 Shen Chou, Ming dynasty:
Lofty Mount Lu.
The National Palace Museum, Taipei.

139 T'ang Yin, Ming dynasty:
Soughing Pines on a Mountain Path.
The National Palace Museum, Taipei.

140 Ch'en Ch'un, Ming dynasty:
Flowers.
The National Palace Museum, Taipei.

141 Ch'en Hung-shou, Ming dynasty:
Rock of Inebriation.
The National Palace Museum, Taipei.

142 Tung Ch'i-ch'ang, Ming dynasty:
Discussing Connoisseurship at Feng-ching.
The National Palace Museum, Taipei.

143 Shih-t'ao, Ch'ing dynasty:
Album of Flowers.
Shanghai Museum.

144 Wang Shih-min, Ch'ing dynasty:
After Wang Wei's 'Clearing Snow on the River.'
The National Palace Museum, Taipei.

145 Wang Chien, Ch'ing dynasty:
After a Landscape by Chao Meng-fu.
The National Palace Museum, Taipei.

146 Wang Hui, Ch'ing dynasty:
Mountains, Streams and Autumn-tinted Trees.
The National Palace Museum, Taipei.

147 Wang Yüan-ch'i, Ch'ing dynasty:
Living in the Mountains in Summer.
The National Palace Museum, Taipei.

148 Yun Shou-p'ing, Ch'ing dynasty:
Old Trees and Bamboo in the Style of Ni Tsan.
The National Palace Museum, Taipei.

149 Wu Li, Ch'ing dynasty:
After a Landscape by Wu Chen.
The National Palace Museum, Taipei.

150 Shih-t'ao, Ch'ing dynasty:
Gazing at the Waterfall on Mount Lu.
Sen-oku Hakko kan, Kyoto.

151 Shih-hsi, Ch'ing dynasty:
Tall Mountains, Long Rivers
The National Palace Museum, Taipei.

152 Lang Shih-ning, Ch'ing dynasty:
Album of Flower Paintings.
The National Palace Museum, Taipei.

153 Hua Yen, Ch'ing dynasty:
The Piled Snows of T'ien-shan.
The Palace Museum, Beijing.

154 Lo P'ing, Ch'ing dynasty:
Portrait of I-an.
Private collection.

155 Kao Feng-han, Ch'ing dynasty:
Peonies.
Osaka Municipal Museum.

156 Chin Nung, Ch'ing dynasty:
Picking Water-chestnuts.
Shanghai Museum.

157 Chao Chih-ch'ien, Ch'ing dynasty:
Album of Flowers.
Private collection.

158 Jen I, Ch'ing dynasty:
Wisteria, Bamboo and Narcissus.
Private collection.

■ Afterword *for the English Edition*

This book was written with the intention of providing those interested in Chinese painting a gateway to its enjoyment and understanding. It is divided into two parts. The first half of the book discusses different aspects of appreciation, while the second provides a brief history of Chinese painting. The goal is to help guide the viewer through a process that takes one from the understanding of a single painting to understanding of the entire tradition. I have spent most of my professional career in the National Palace Museum in Taiwan and in the course of my work, I have often been asked how one should look at a particular painting, where its subtle points may lie, or its relationship to some other painting—questions ranging from the manner in which one appreciates a painting to matters concerning its history. In the company of friends, one can answer such questions as they arise, but over time I came to realize that there may be a place for a book that can approach the issue more systematically.

The appreciation of beauty is a feature of all peoples and all societies, and painting gives form to beauty in a manner that is direct and universally understood. The single fundamental condition is that a painting must be seen. With this in mind, I have written this book with the idea of "looking" at Chinese paintings and certainly this is something more easily done today, with museums and fine art publications, than in traditional times. One begins the process of understanding painting by first looking. I hope that this book will help train the reader to look, to move on to a deeper appreciation of Chinese painting with eyes that know how to look.

I offer my sincerest gratitude to Nigensha for publishing the English Edition of my book. Already as a student practicing calligraphy, I knew of Nigensha's publications, with their excellent reproductions of famous works of Chinese calligraphy. Shortly after I began working at the National Palace Museum in 1976, Nigensha began to collaborate with the Museum in the making of fine quality facsimile reproductions of famous paintings and calligraphy. For well over a decade now, staff members from Nigensha have come to Taiwan and I have had the honor of watching these people at work. Their diligence and commitment to excellence sets a standard that should be a model for all of us. That same diligence was maintained in translating this book into Japanese and English, during the course of which a number of flaws in the original text were discovered and corrected. For this, I am extremely grateful. Nigensha possesses a unique repository of high-quality photographic materials of Chinese paintings. Their use in the Japanese and English editions has resulted in a greatly improved version of my original book, with beautiful, clear images that facilitate the book's fundamental goal of allowing the viewer to take a close look at Chinese painting. For this, too, I offer my deepest thanks. As a museum curator and teacher of art and art history, I hope that this book will serve to introduce Chinese painting in a manner that has not yet been done in the West. I close with a word of appreciation for the Stone Studio for their excellent translation and for Mr. Arai Yuzo of the Art Editorial Department of Nigensha, whose hard work and diligence have been instrumental in this edition's publication.

Wang Yao-t'ing

WANG YAO-T'ING

Wang Yao-t'ing was born in the town of Lu-kang, in Chang-hua County, Taiwan, in 1943. He graduated from the Art Department of Taiwan Normal University in 1972 and received a Masters degree in Chinese art history from the History Department of National Taiwan University in 1977. Wang Yao-t'ing has been a lecturer at Soochow University and Ching-hua University, in addition to working as a researcher in the Calligraphy and Painting Department of the National Palace Museum. Among his numerous publications are *Hua-hsia chih mei—hui-hua [The Beauty of Chinese Art—Painting]* (Taipei: Yu-shih shu-chu, 1985), *Huang-ti ch'u-yu [The Emperor's Tour]* (Taipei: Taiwan shu-tien, 1984), *Shan-shui-hua 1, 2, 3 [Landscape Painting 1, 2, 3]* (Taipei: Hsiung-shih t'u-shu, 1984), *Chung-kuo hui-hua [Chinese Painting]* (Taipei: Taiwan shu-tien, 1992) and a number of scholarly articles on Chinese painting.